CONTENTS

Encouraging Interest

Help students to develop an understanding and appreciation for different artists and types of art by highlighting a variety of artists each month. Display examples of an artist's artwork and have students study and duplicate their style. In addition, encourage students to visit art museums online or visit local art galleries.

Student Sketchbook Ideas

Give each student a large sketchbook in which to explore art techniques, create designs, collect examples of artwork they admire and challenge their thinking about art. Encourage students to add to their sketchbook at least once a week.

Coloring Pages

These pages are intended to give students practice in using different elements of design.

Rubrics and Checklists

Use the rubrics in this book to assess student learning.

Learning Logs

In addition to a sketchbook have students keep a learning log as an effective way for students to organize their thoughts and ideas about art concepts presented. Learning logs can include the following kinds of entries:

- teacher journal prompts
- questions that arise
- labeled diagrams
- student personal reflections
- connections discovered

Art Glossary

List new art vocabulary and their meanings on chart paper for students' reference during activities.

Elements of Design: Color Activities 2	Working with Elements of Design 57
Elements of Design: Value Activities 13	Art Discussion Prompts: Looking at a Painting 62
Elements of Design: Shape Activities 16	Artist-Inspired Art Ideas 63
Elements of Design: Line Activities 26	A Portrait of a Famous Artist 66
Elements of Design: Form Activities 32	Similarities and Differences 67
	Direct Draw 68
	Sketchbook Drawing Ideas 69
Elements of Design: Texture Activities 43	Seasonal Art Ideas 70
	Art Rubrics 72
Elements of Design: Space Activities 53	Art Web Sites for Students 76
	Art Glossary 77
	Student Art Certificates 80

ELEMENTS OF DESIGN: COLOR

Activity 1: Creating Mood

What you need:
- Coloring materials such as pencil crayons, pastels, watercolors or crayons • Paper

What to do:

1. Ask students if they think color can create a mood, or strong feeling. Discuss how. Brainstorm ways that warm colors can affect mood and ways that cool colors can affect mood.

2. Have students create a picture or design with an overall mood. Themes that students can choose to illustrate include:
   - a fantasy world or creature
   - an underwater environment
   - a futuristic world

3. When they have completed their artwork, have students write a journal entry to explain the mood they were trying to create and how they chose and used colors to do it.

Activity 2: Complementary Colors

What you need:
- Paper
- Watercolors
- Paintbrushes
- Rulers
- Black markers
- Pencil

What to do:

1. Review with students the concept of complementary colors. These are colors that are directly opposite each other on the color wheel. For example, red and green or blue and orange.

2. Next, tell students that they are going to create an abstract complementary painting.

3. Instruct students to produce a design of black outlines of overlapping abstract shapes. Encourage students to use spirals, diagonals and other types of lines.

4. Have students choose and use complementary colors to paint the sections of their design.

THE COLOR WHEEL

The **Color Wheel** is a color circle based on red, yellow and blue.

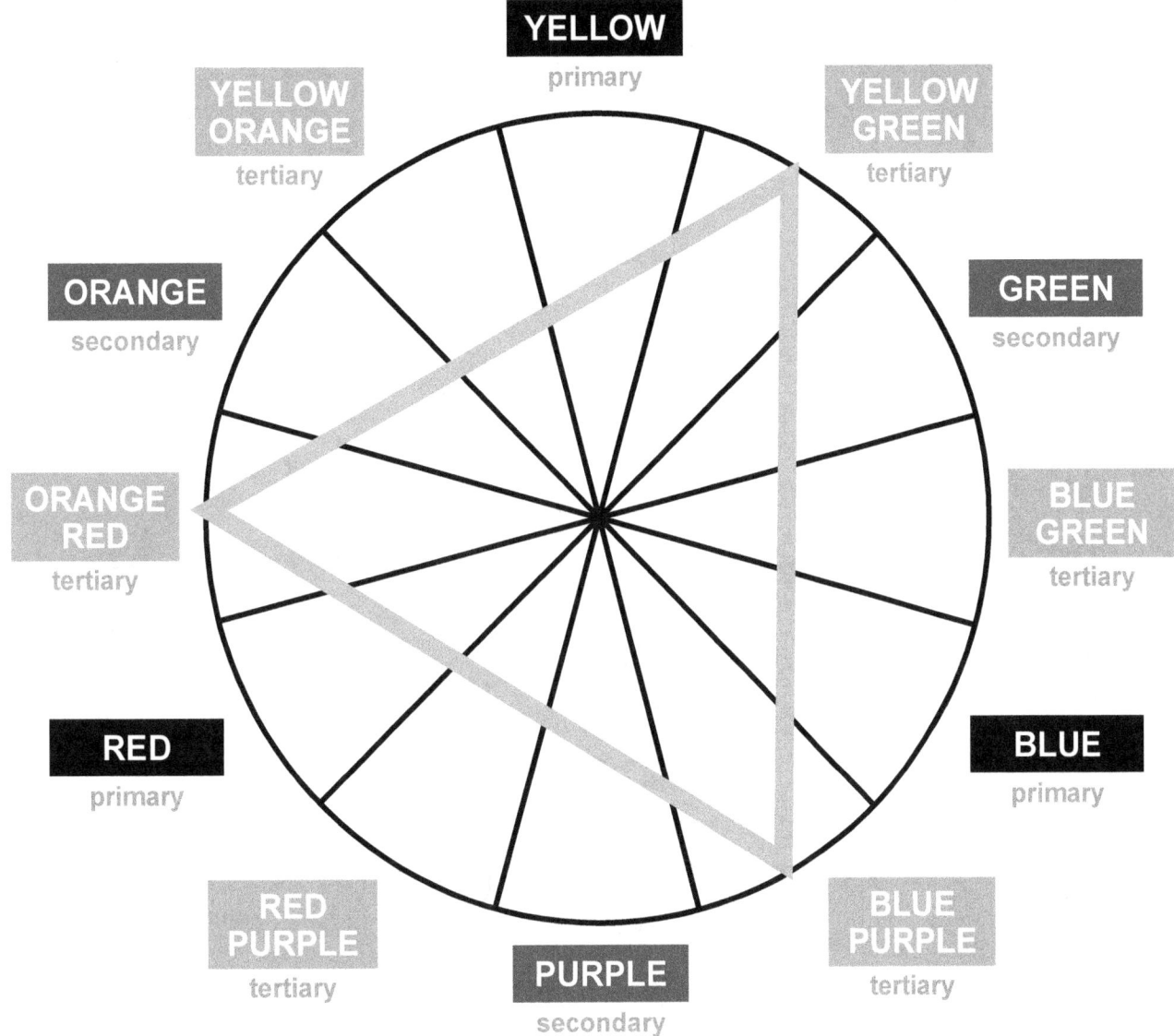

The **primary colors** are red, yellow and blue. Primary colors cannot be mixed or created by any combination of other colors.

The **secondary colors** are purple, green and orange. These colors are created by mixing the primary colors.

The **tertiary colors** are created by mixing a primary and a secondary color.

Complementary colors are any two colors that are opposite each other on the color wheel, such as red and green or blue and orange. In theory, opposite colors create maximum contrast.

THE COLOR WHEEL

The color wheel is _____
_____

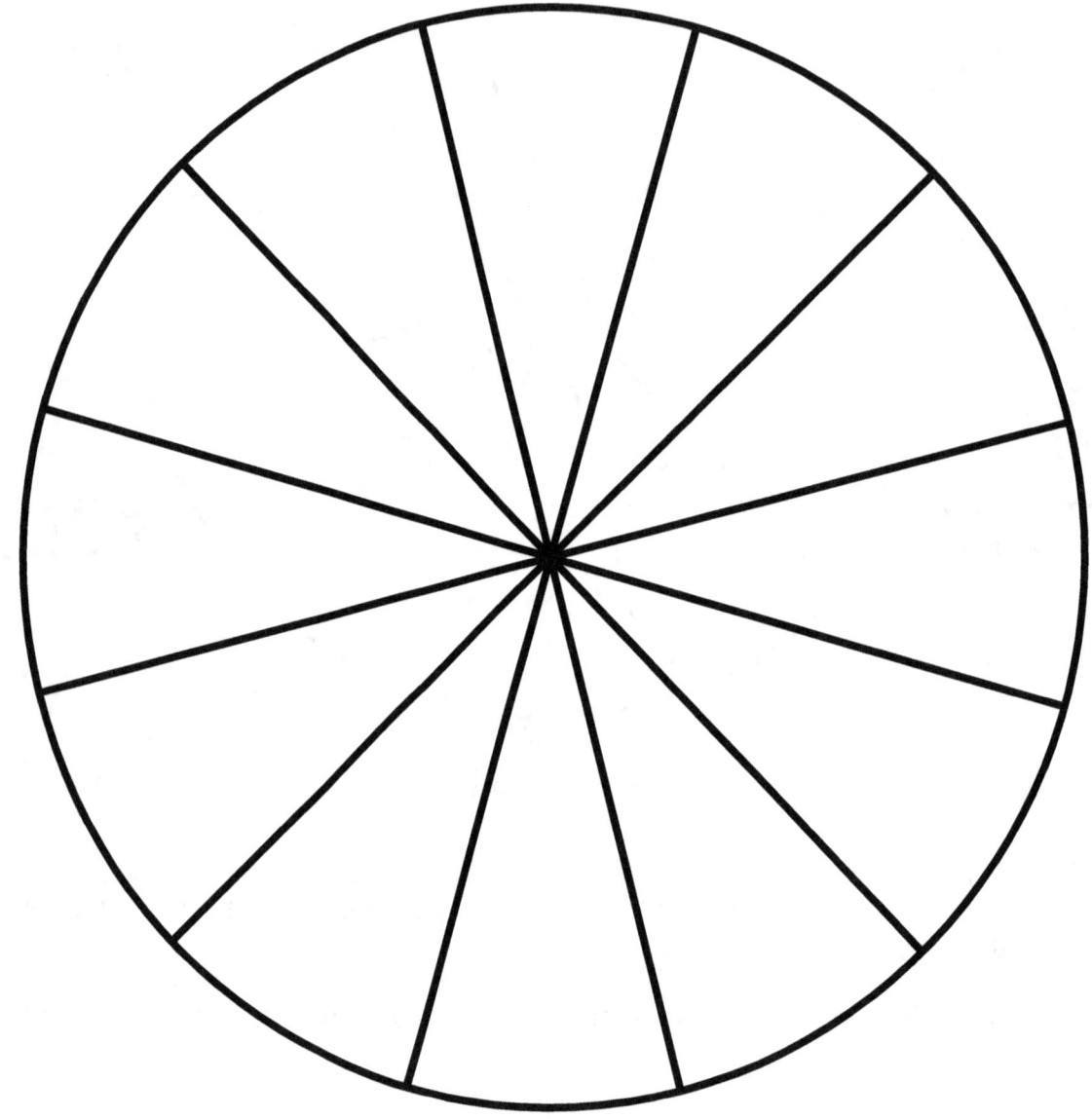

THE COLOR WHEEL

Primary Colors

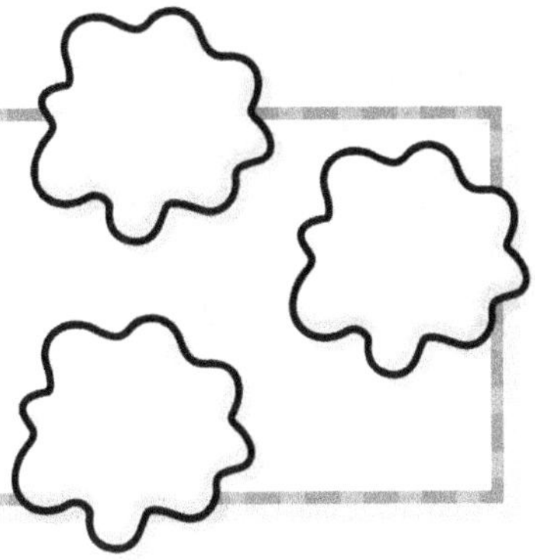

_____
_____

Secondary Colors

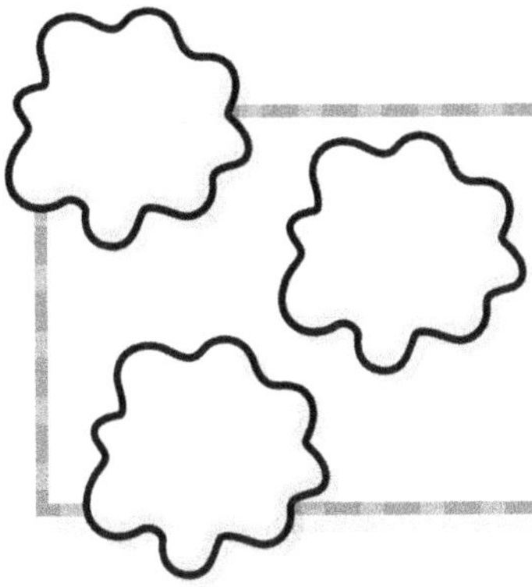

_____
_____

Tertiary Colors

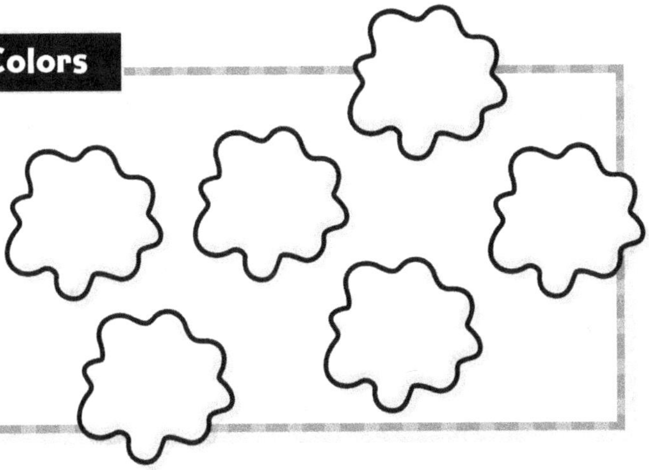

_____
_____
_____
_____

Complementary Colors

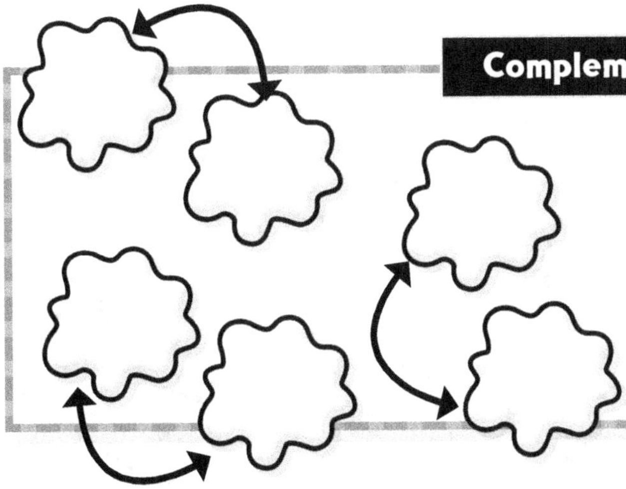

_____
_____
_____
_____

CONTRASTING COLORS

Contrast: A principle of design where light colors are used next to dark colors.

Test different color combinations on another piece of paper. Then copy the combinations that best match the descriptions below.

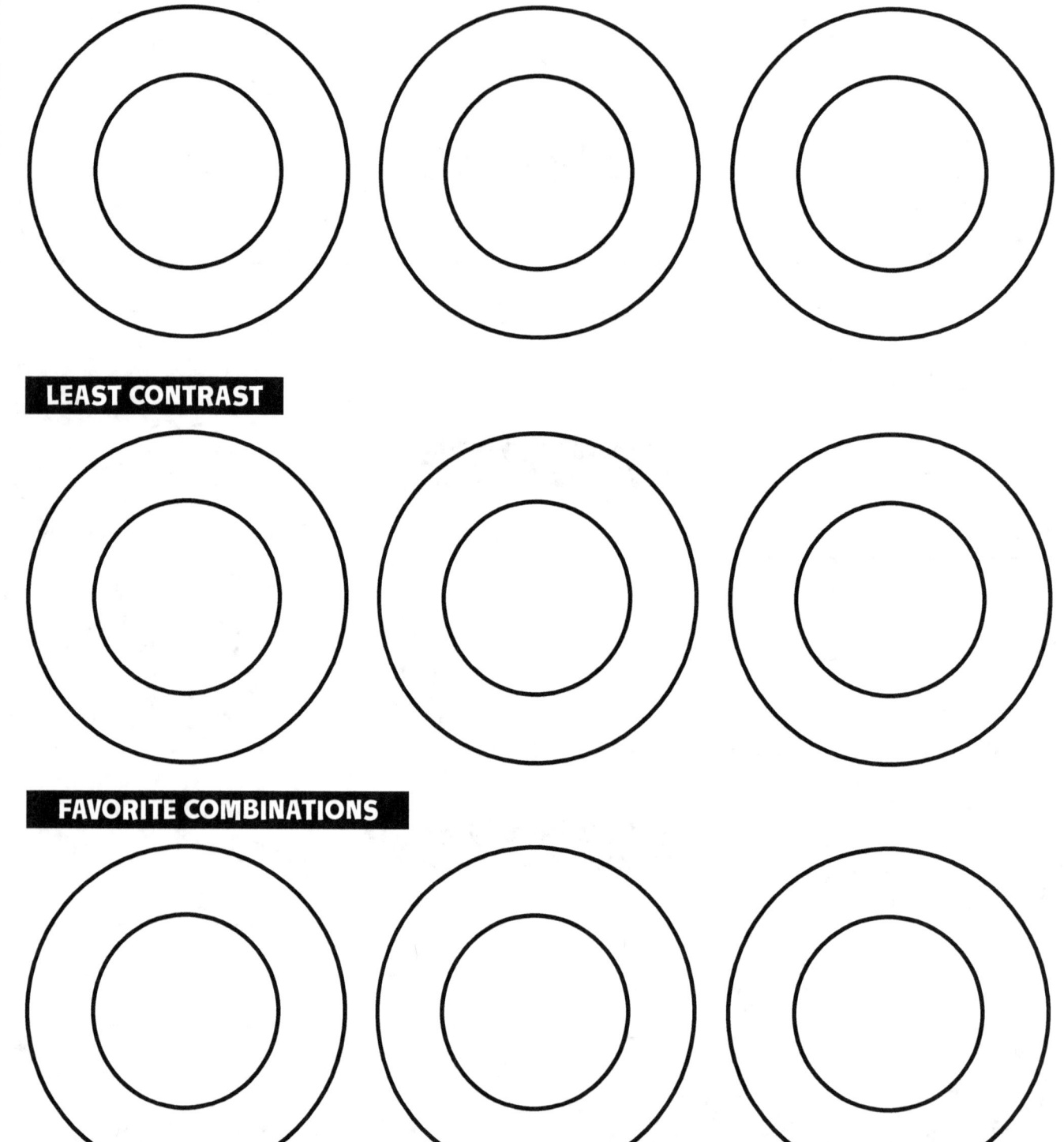

COLORS AND THEIR MEANINGS

RED: energy, excitement, momentum, strength, power, warmth, love, anger, danger, fire, aggression, passion

YELLOW: joy, happiness, hopefulness, optimism, imagination, sunshine, summer, gold, dishonesty, fear, betrayal, envy, illness

BLUE: harmony, peace, calm, steadiness, unity, trust, confidence, cleanliness, order, security, loyalty, sky, water, cold, technology, sadness

GREEN: nature, environment, health, good luck, renewal, youth, vitality, spring, generosity, fertility, jealousy, inexperience, hardship

ORANGE: energy, balance, warmth, enthusiasm, expansiveness, glitz, attention-grabbing

PURPLE: royalty, spirituality, nobility, mystery, transformation, wisdom, enlightenment, cruelty, arrogance, mourning

GRAY: safety, dependability, intelligence, modesty, maturity, depression, boredom, old-fashioned, practical

WHITE: admiration, purity, minimalism, cleanliness, peace, innocence, youth, birth, winter, snow, virtue, hygiene

BROWN: earth, home, outdoors, trustworthiness, comfort, staying power, strength, simplicity, calm

BLACK: power, dominance, formality, elegance, wealth, mystery, terror, evil, anonymity, unhappiness, sadness, remorse, death

COLOR IN ADVERTISING

In advertising, the colors chosen and the way they are used can help to sell a product or convey a message. Look at different advertisements in magazines. Choose one advertisement and explain, using your own ideas and the meanings of different colors, how it uses color to sell a product or convey a message.

Advertisement: _____

How does the use of color help to sell the product or convey a message?

_____
_____
_____
_____
_____
_____
_____
_____
_____
_____
_____
_____

COLOR IN ADVERTISING

Create an advertisement for one of the following:

- vacation
- car
- clothing
- perfume
- home
- cereal
- restaurant
- public service announcement (e.g., health, safety)

Think about what color scheme will engage your target audience. What colors should you use to persuade people that they should buy your product or service? If you are creating a public service announcement, what colors will reinforce your message?

What you need:

- Colors and Their Meanings handout
- Paper
- Coloring materials

Plan

What is your advertisement for?

_____
_____
_____

What colors are you going to use and why?

_____
_____
_____
_____

COLOR IN ADVERTISING

Rough Outline

LANDSCAPE ART

Color the picture using only cool colors.

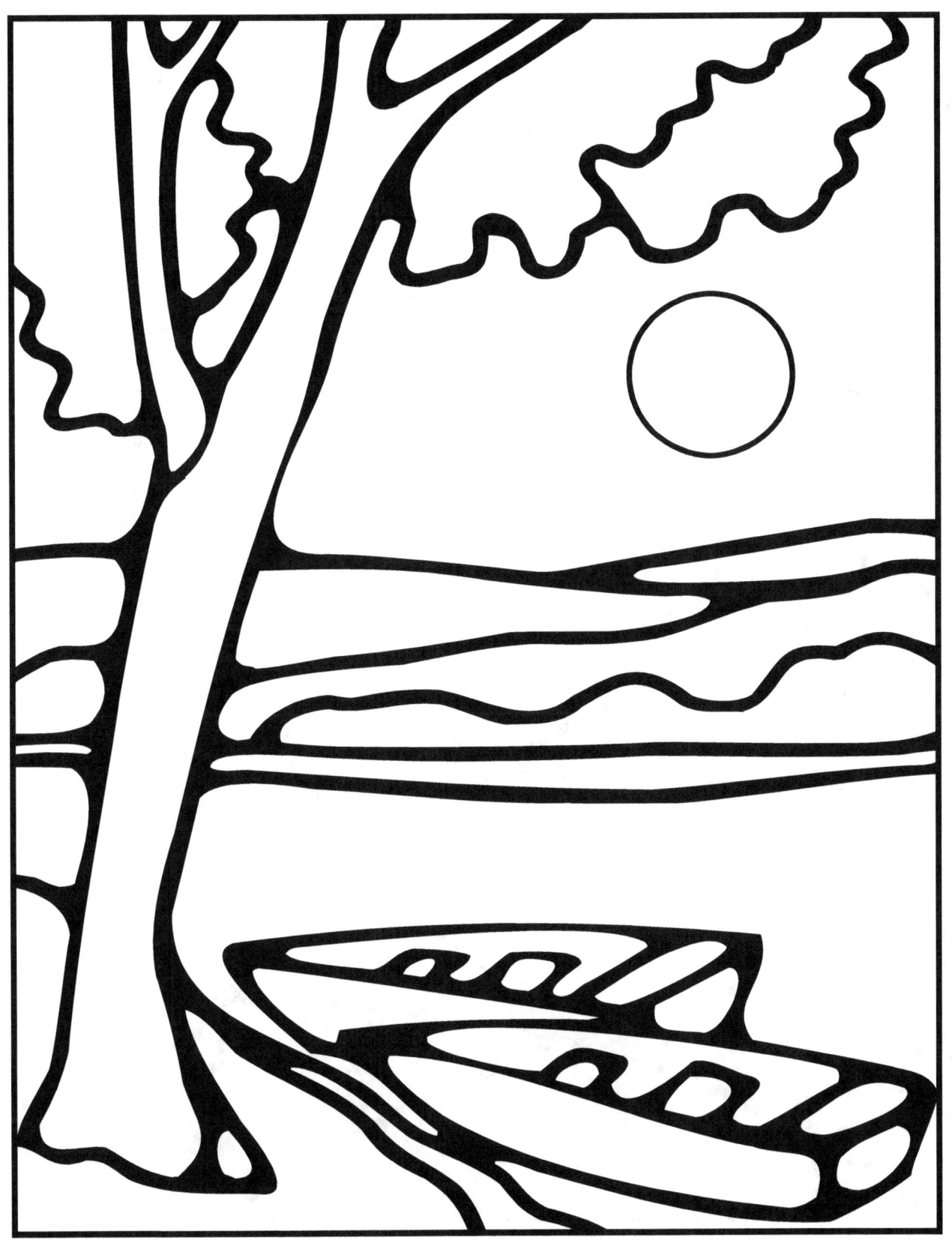

SPORTS FUN

Choose a color scheme and on a separate piece of paper explain your reasoning.

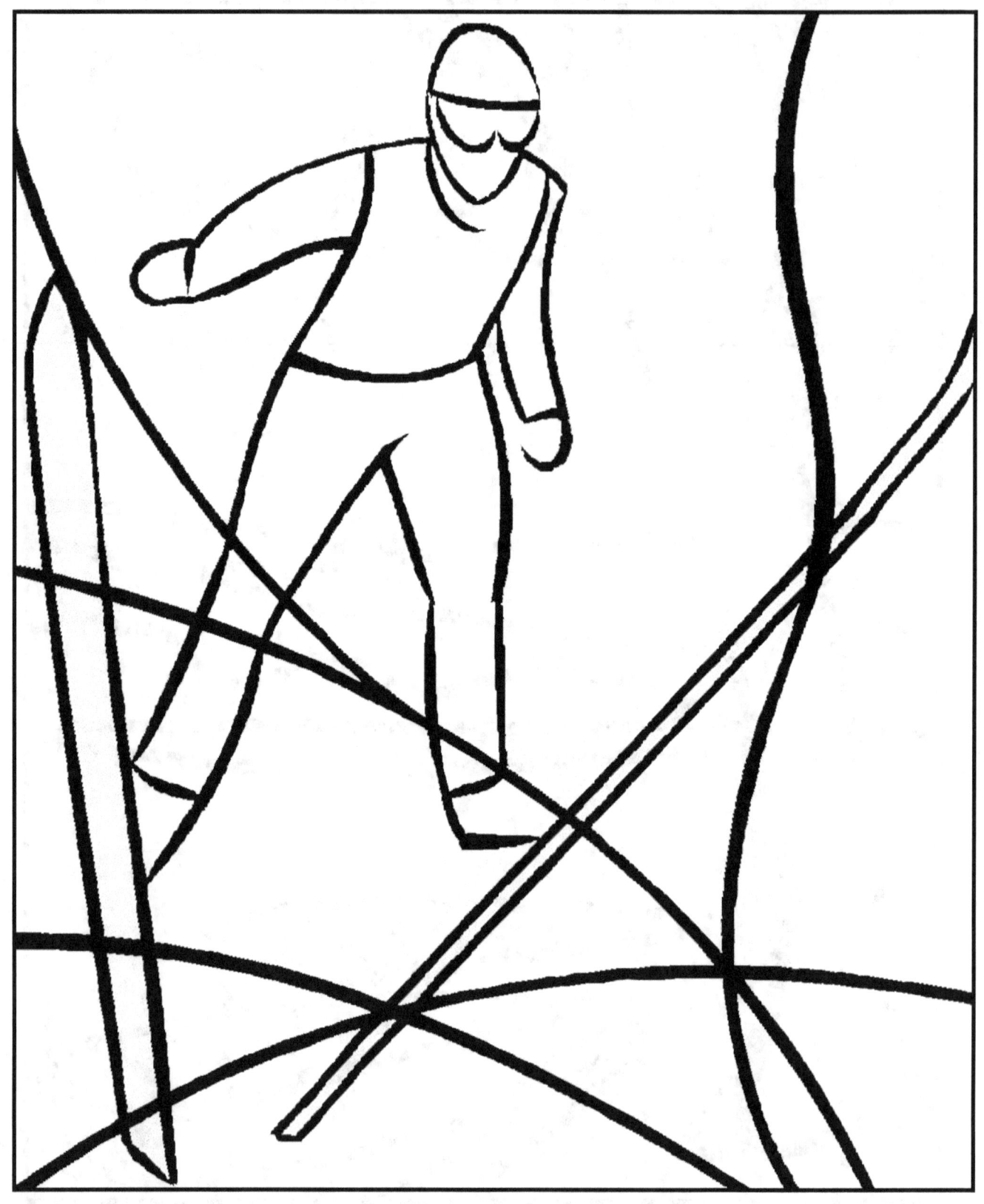

ELEMENTS OF DESIGN: VALUE

Using tempera paint, create shades of the following colors by adding black, a little bit at a time.

	Add one drop of black	**Add a little more...**	**Add a little more...**
RED			
GREEN			
ORANGE			
PURPLE			
BLUE			

ELEMENTS OF DESIGN: VALUE

Using tempera paint, create tints of the following colors by adding white, a little bit at a time.

	Add one drop of white	**Add a little more...**	**Add a little more...**
RED			
GREEN			
ORANGE			
PURPLE			
BLUE			

SPORTS FUN

Color the picture using only tones of black and white.

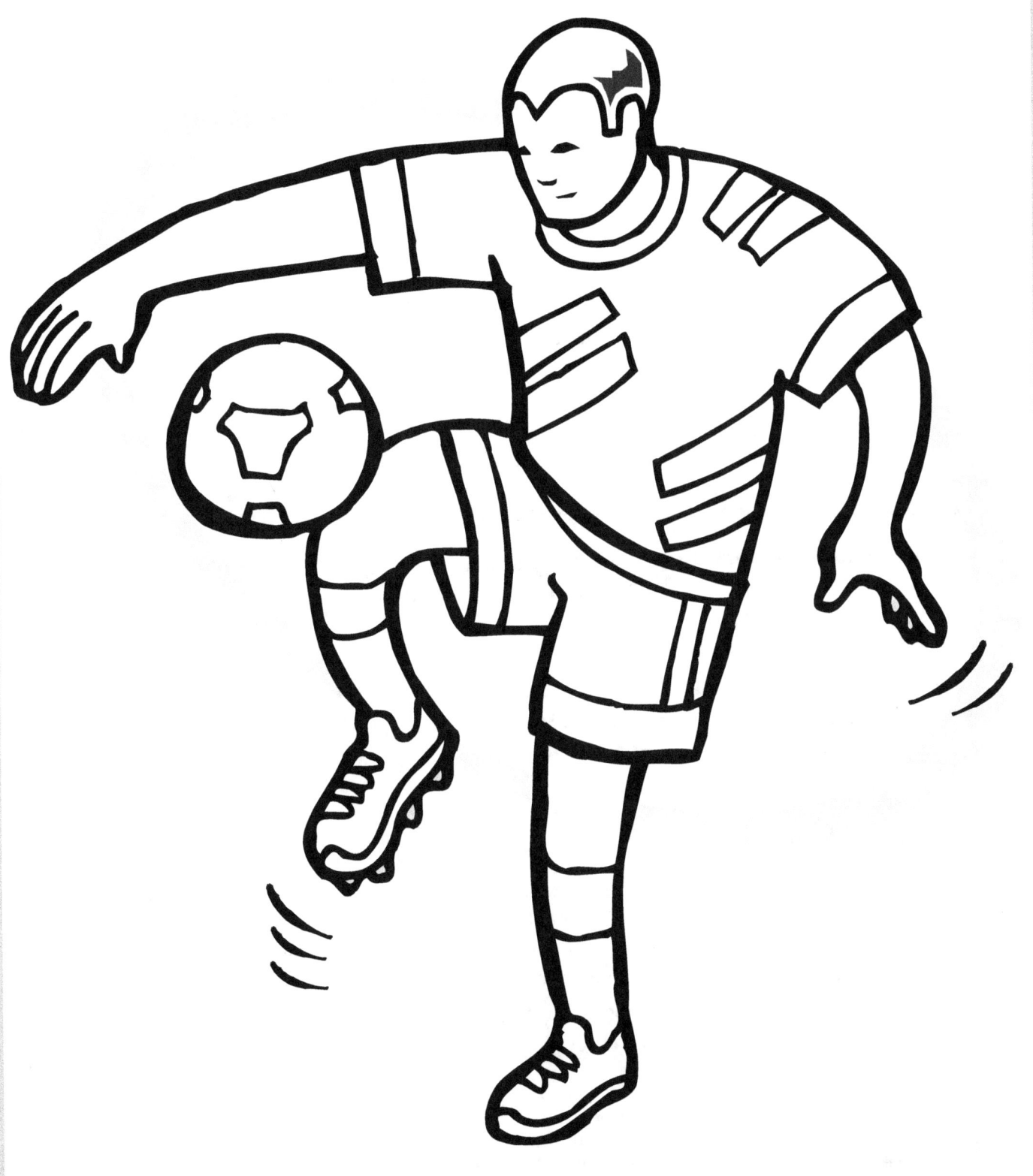

ELEMENTS OF DESIGN: SHAPE

Activity 1: Shape Picture

What you need:
- Black construction paper
- Scissors
- Colored construction paper
- Glue

What to do:
1. Ask students to plan and compose a picture based on geometric shapes.
2. Have students cut out various geometric shapes to use for their picture.
3. Once students have planned a detailed composition, have students glue the shapes onto the black construction paper.

Activity 2: Shape Collage

What you need:
- Paper
- Watercolors
- Paintbrushes
- Rulers
- Black markers
- Pencils

What to do:
1. Instruct students to produce a design of black outlines of overlapping geometric shapes. Encourage students to use a variety of shapes in their design.
2. Next, have students paint sections of the design using a specific approach, such as complementary colors only, secondary colors only, different tints, and so on.
3. When students have finished, discuss with them their approach to their artwork.

SHAPE HUNT

Find and list places where you see or use the following geometric shapes in everyday life.

Circle	Octagon

Triangle	Trapezoid

Square	Hexagon

Rectangle	Oval

ORGANIC SHAPE HUNT

Organic Shape: Non-geometric or free-flowing shape.

Look around and draw different organic shapes you see.

TERRIFIC TANGRAMS

A tangram is an ancient Chinese puzzle made from seven geometric shapes. The objective is to form a specific shape with these seven pieces.

1. Carefully cut out the tangram shapes below.
2. Use the tangram shapes to construct an animal, person or thing. Your new shape design must contain all the pieces, which may not overlap.

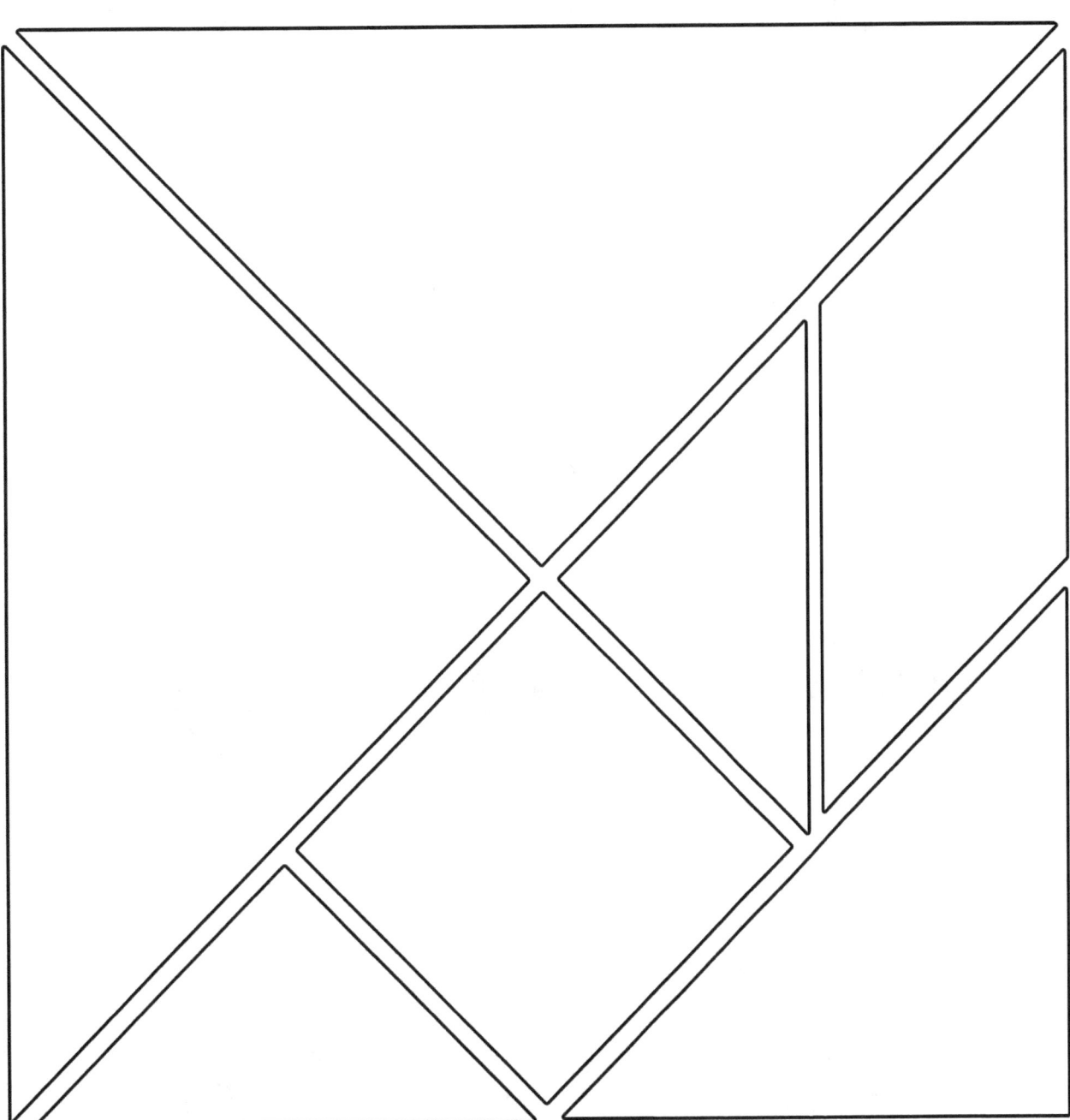

TERRIFIC TANGRAM CHALLENGE

How many of these tangram animal puzzles can you solve?

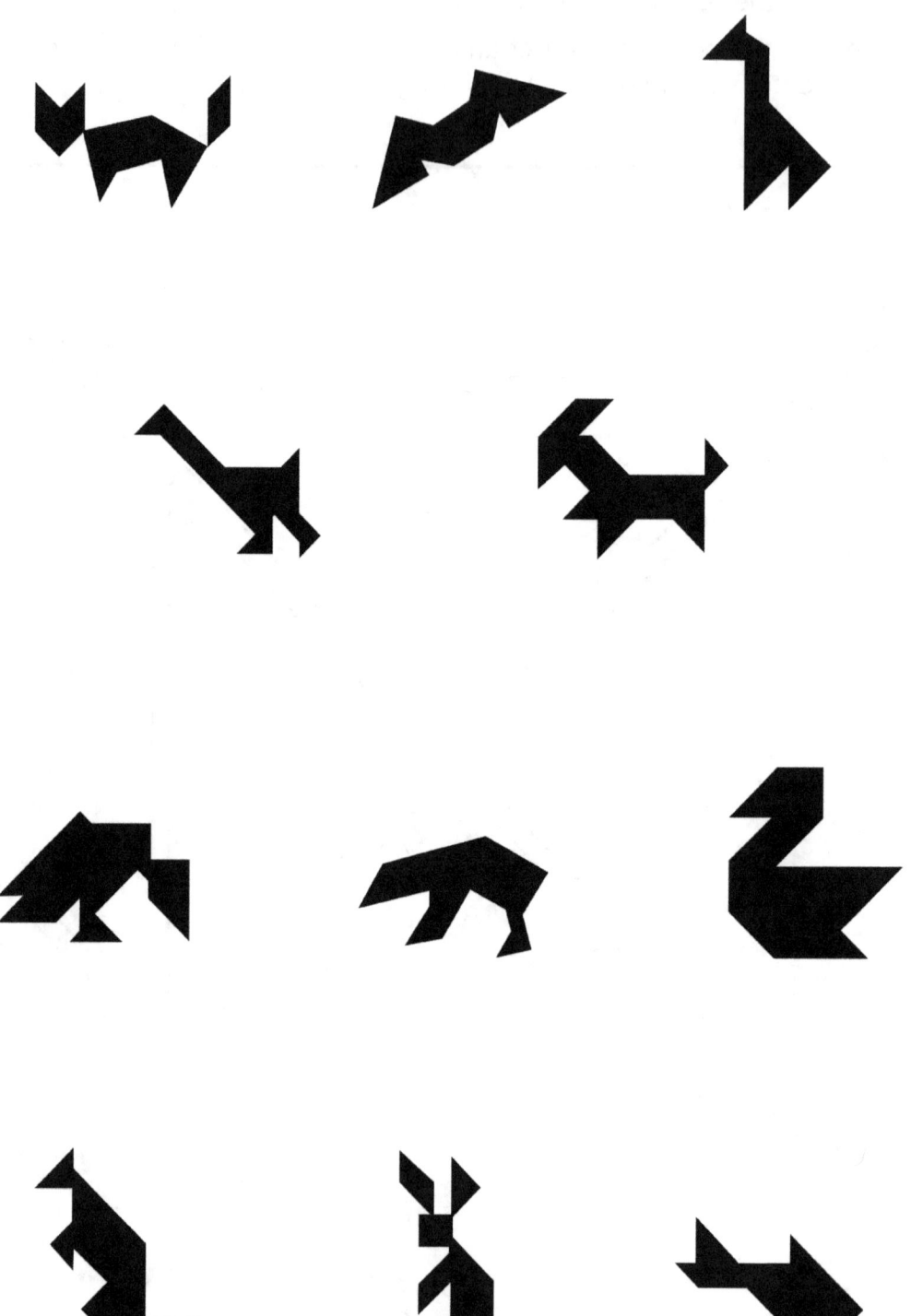

TERRIFIC TANGRAM CHALLENGE

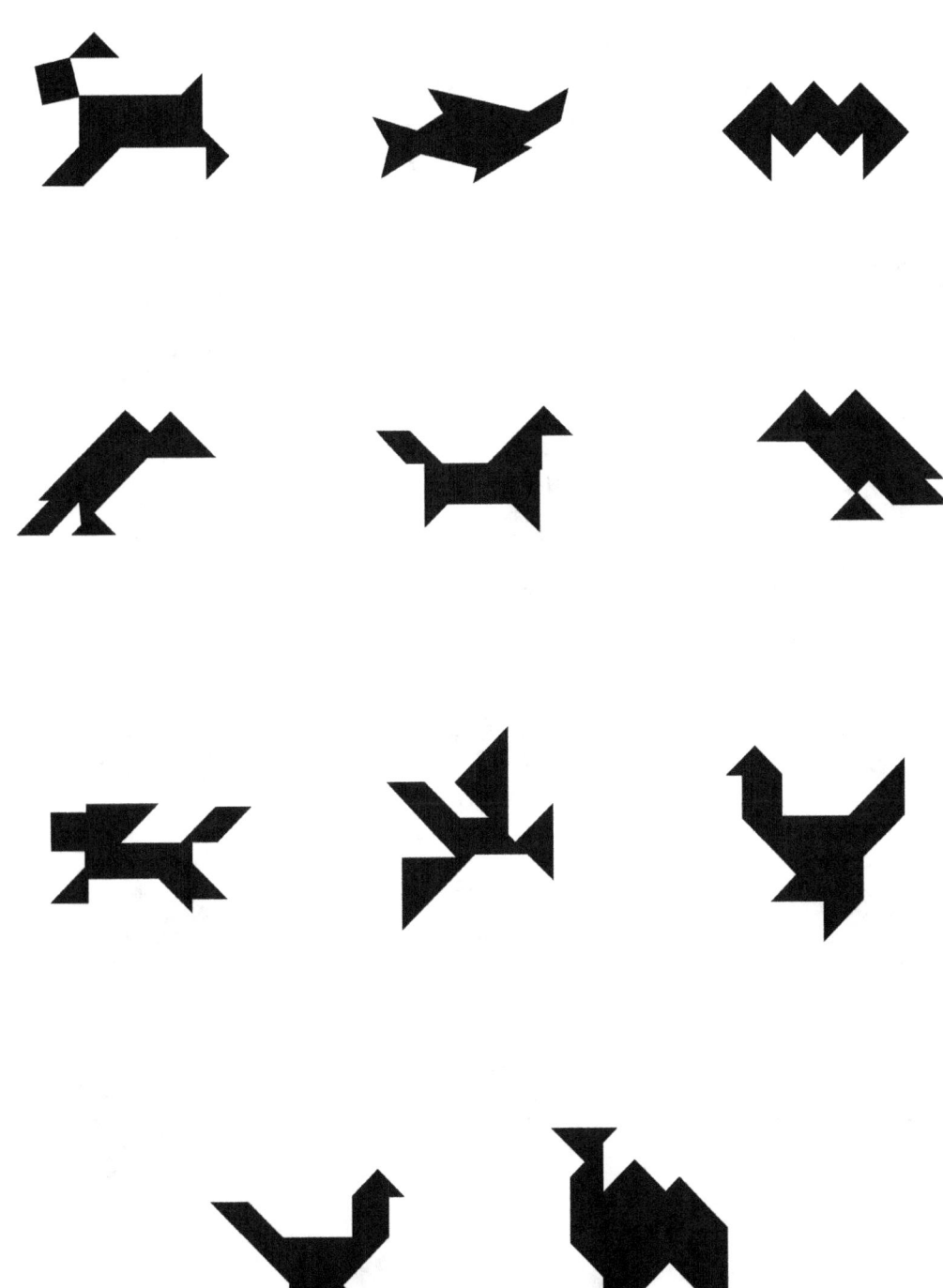

TERRIFIC TANGRAM CHALLENGE SOLUTIONS

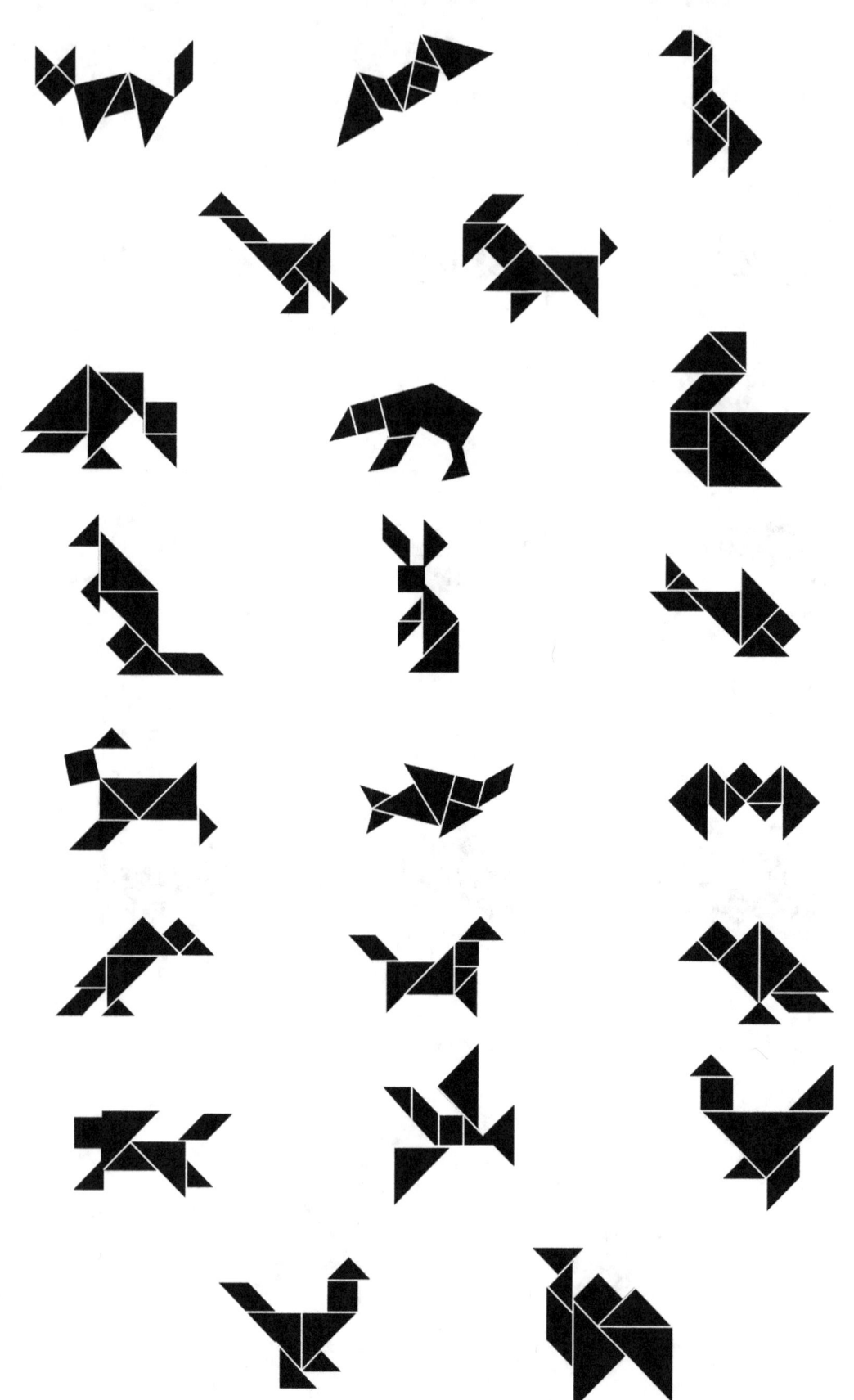

GEOMETRIC DESIGN

Color the geometric design using different shades of only one color.

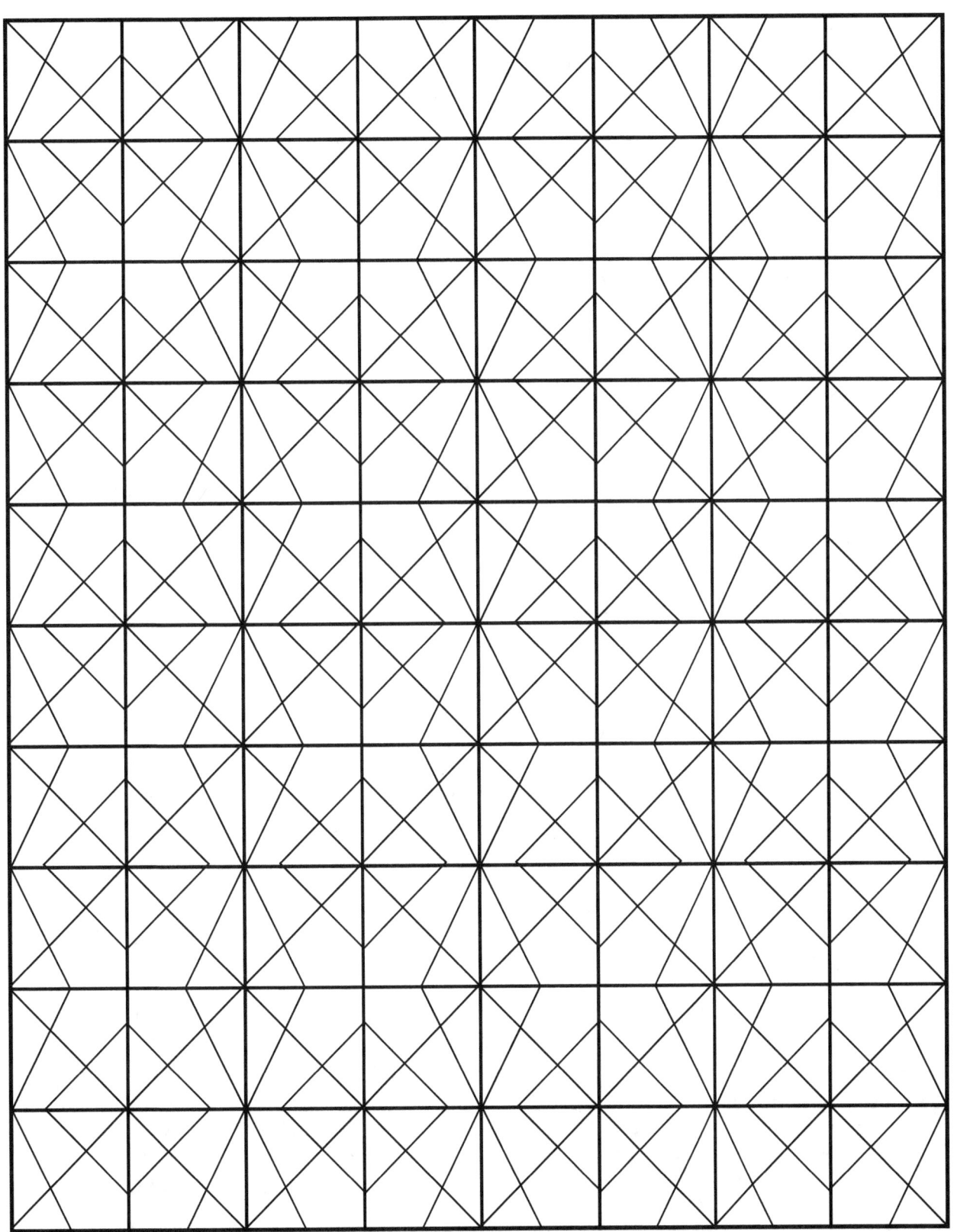

GEOMETRIC DESIGN

Color the geometric design using primary colors.

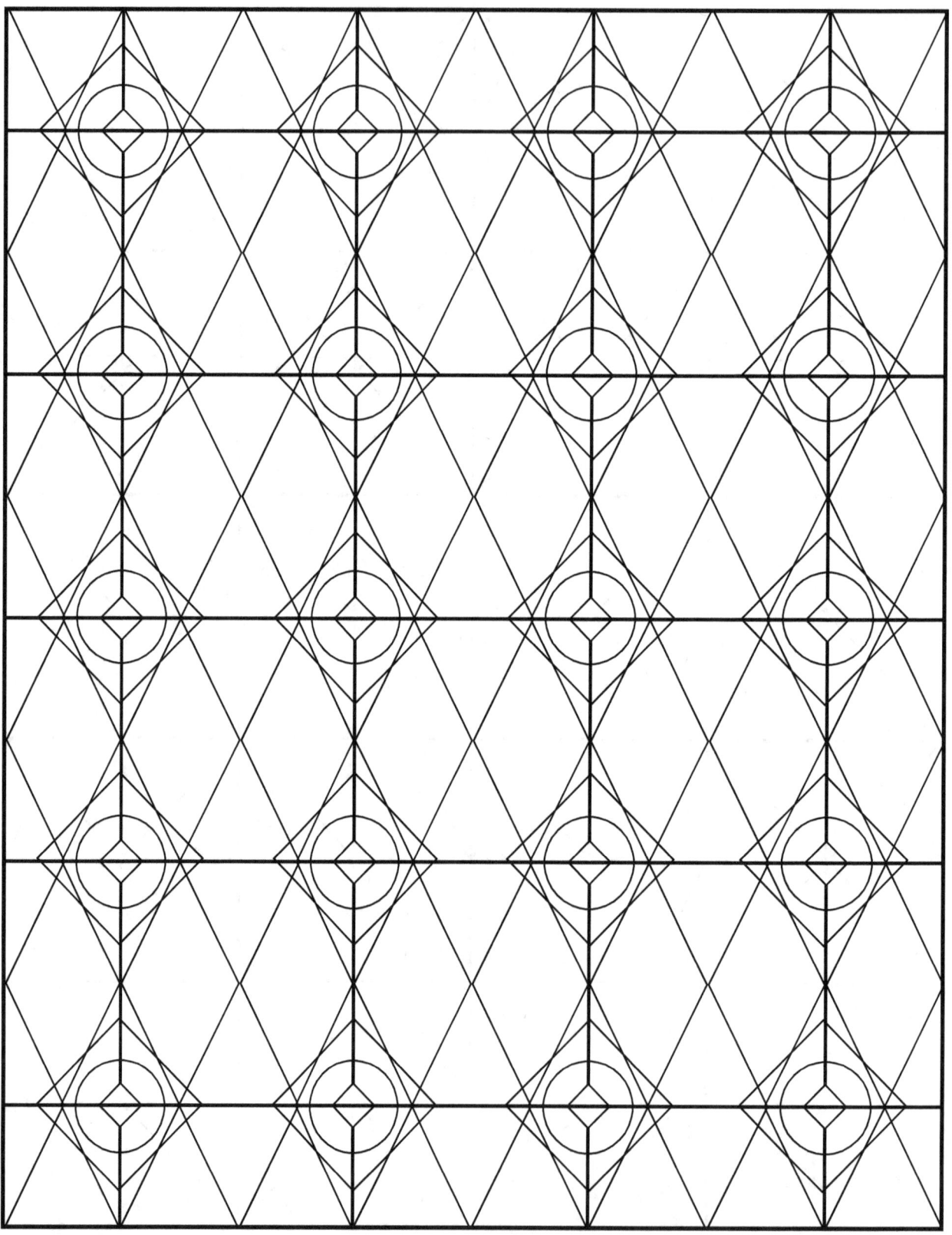

GEOMETRIC DESIGN

Color the geometric design using tertiary colors.

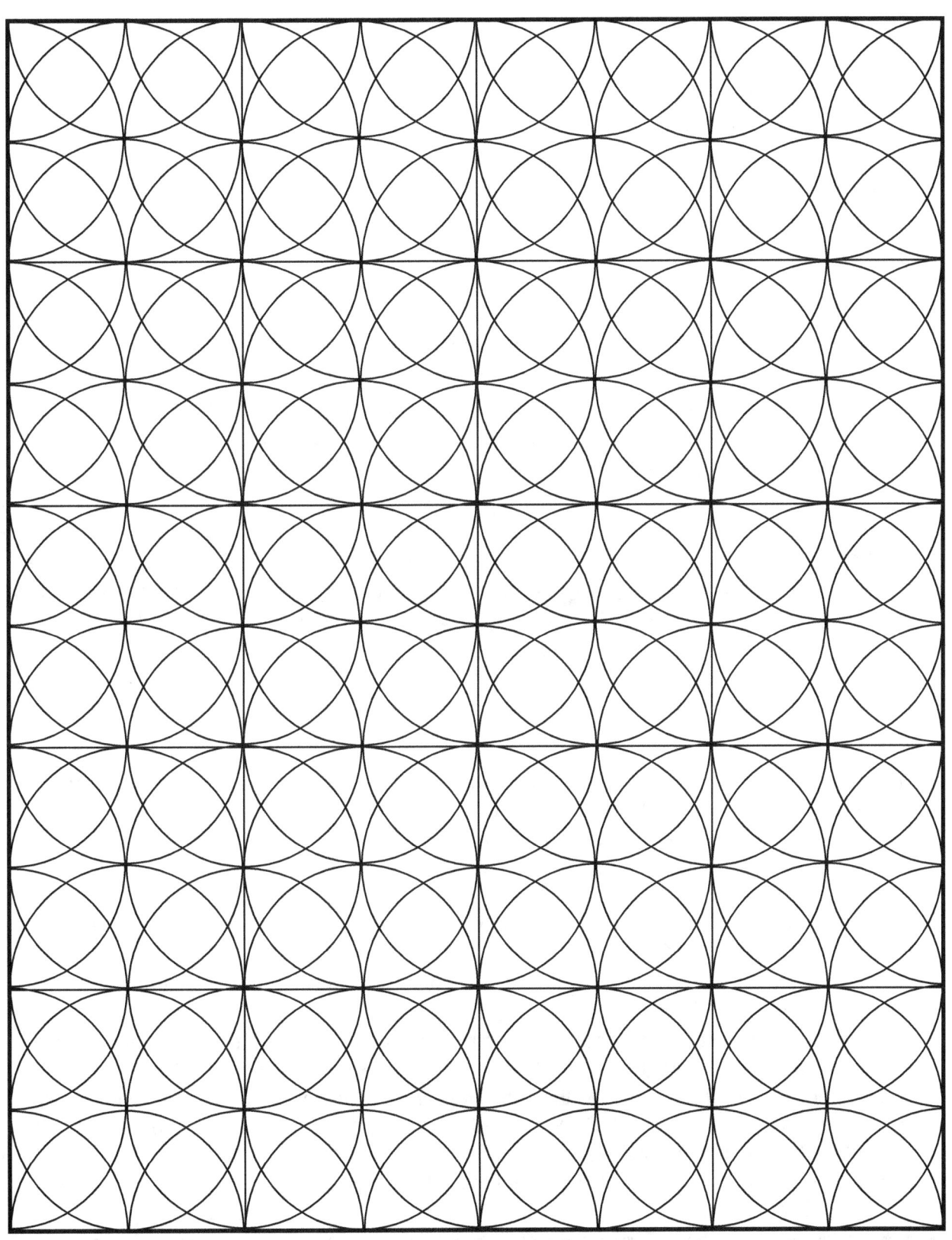

ELEMENTS OF DESIGN: LINE

Activity 1: Outlining Objects

What you need:
- Crayons
- Pastels
- Paint and paintbrushes
- A variety of everyday objects such as scissors, drinking glasses, cans, or toothbrush
- Paper
- Chalk
- Pencil crayons

What to do:
1. Demonstrate for students how to trace the contour of various objects to produce a pleasing line composition.
2. Invite students to trace various objects, overlapping them to produce their own line compositions. Encourage students to use assorted drawing materials and colors and to notice the types of lines created by each.

Activity 2: Contour Drawing

What you need:
- Paper
- Small fruits
- HB pencil

What to do:
1. Explain to students that they will be completing a contour drawing of a small fruit such as a pear or banana. Review the term contour drawing.
2. Have students begin by placing the fruit of their choice near the paper. Students may find it helpful to strive to make their drawings the same size as the actual fruit.
3. Then encourage students to begin their contour drawing. They should choose a point on the edge of the fruit and follow its contour with their eyes, allowing their hand to copy the shape of the fruit onto the paper.
4. Caution students not to rush. They should try to draw every curve, including strong lines on the fruit such as a fold or crease.
5. Remind students that the purpose of this activity is to practice getting their hand and eye to do the same thing, by judging the size and shape of the edges the student can see.
6. Once done, have students review their drawings and consider whether their drawings match the real-life shapes of the fruit. Discuss whether the proportions are correct and whether enough details were included.
7. Repeat this drawing activity using different everyday objects.

ELEMENTS OF DESIGN: LINE

Activity 3: Blind Contour Drawing

What you need:
- Paper • HB pencil

What to do:

1. Explain to students that they will complete a blind contour drawing of their hand. Review the terms contour drawing and blind contour drawing.
2. Have students begin by placing their pencils near the bottom edge of the paper.
3. Then encourage students to begin drawing. They should look at the edge of their wrist and slowly follow the contour of one hand with their eyes, allowing the other hand to slowly and carefully draw the line they see on the paper. Remind students to keep their eyes on the hand they are drawing, not the hand that is moving! Encourage students not to rush and to record every curve and bump they see. If they get to a fold or crease in the skin, they should follow it in and then back out to the side.
4. Have students review their drawings and comment on the accuracy of their drawings. What surprised them about this activity and the results?
5. Repeat the activity using students' running shoes.

Activity 4: Sgraffito

What you need:
- Paper (untextured)
- Crayons
- Paintbrushes
- Thick tempera paint
- Objects that scratch, such as, toothpicks, tongue depressors, combs, coins and plastic utensils

What to do:

1. Invite students to draw broad bands of color, using crayons, on a piece of paper that has a smooth surface. Remind students to apply pressure on the crayons as they draw.
2. Once completed, have students paint over the entire paper with the black tempera paint.
3. After the paint dries encourage students to scratch designs onto the paper using the objects. This technique is called sgraffito.

ELEMENTS OF DESIGN: LINE

Activity 5: Rhythm and Line

What you need:
- Crayons
- Pastels
- Different types of music
- Paper
- Chalk
- Pencil crayons

What to do:

1. Choose and play a piece of music for students and have them trace the rhythm of the music with a finger in the air. Ask them to describe the line their finger creates.
2. Now, have students draw the line that represents the rhythm of the music using the material(s) and color(s) of their choice. Have students add more such lines above and below the first line.
3. Repeat the activity with different types of music and discuss as a class why students chose the types of lines and colors they did for each.

Activity 6: Experiment with Lines

What you need:
- Assorted colors of tissue paper
- Water
- Shallow pan
- White paper

What to do:

1. Have students moisten pieces of tissue paper by dipping them in a shallow pan of water.
2. Next, lay the wet tissue paper onto white paper in interesting arrangements.
3. Allow the tissue paper to dry.
4. Once the tissue paper has dried, have students outline the interesting shapes or patterns that result.

LINES, LINES, LINES!

Draw examples of the following lines.

Thin Lines

Thick Lines

Wavy Lines

Dotted Lines

Zigzag Lines

FLOWER LINE DESIGNS

Fill in the sections of the picture using at least five different types of lines and your own color scheme.

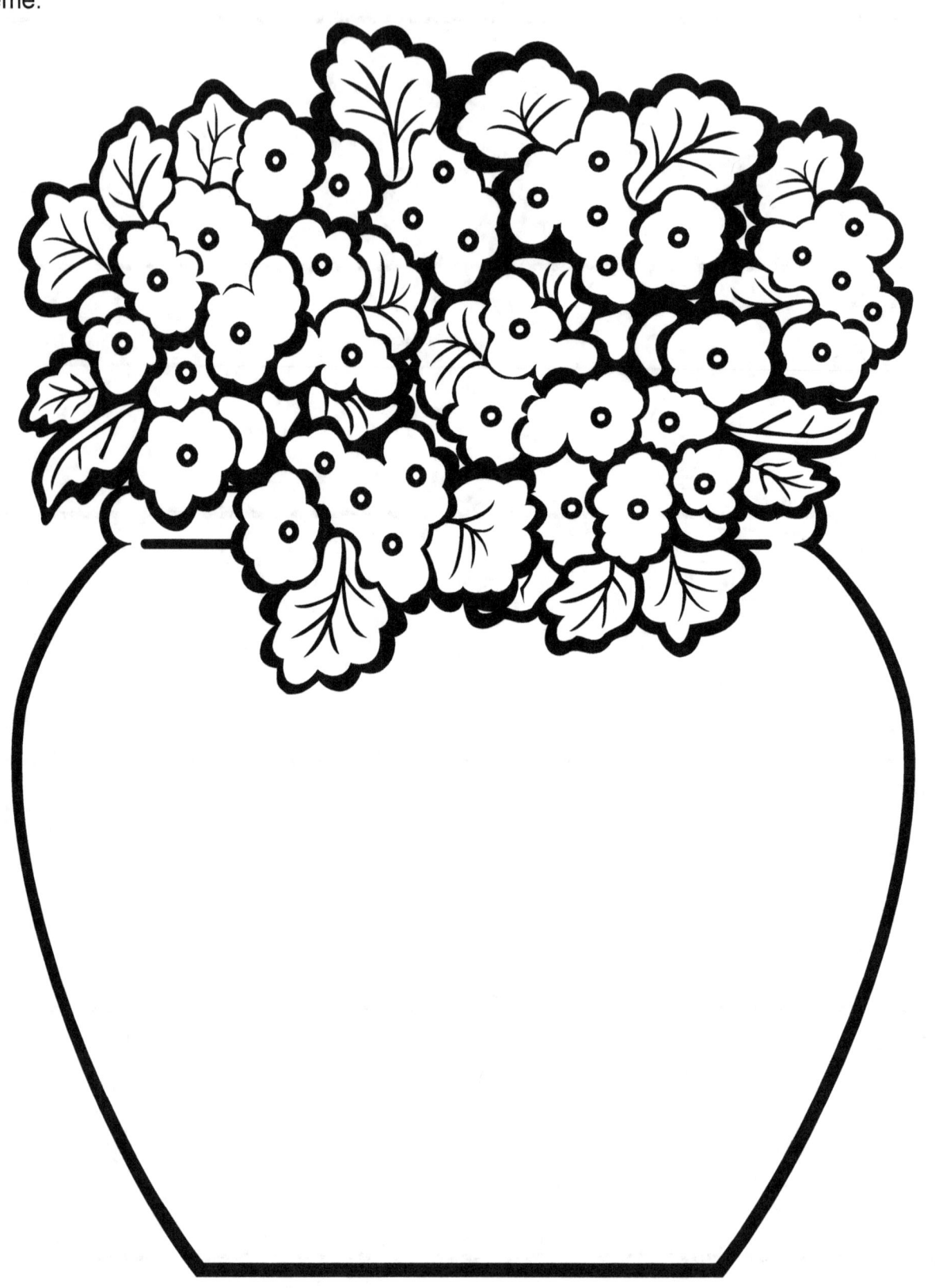

THINKING ABOUT LINE

Color the picture. **BRAIN STRETCH:** Why do you think the artist used curved lines to represent water?

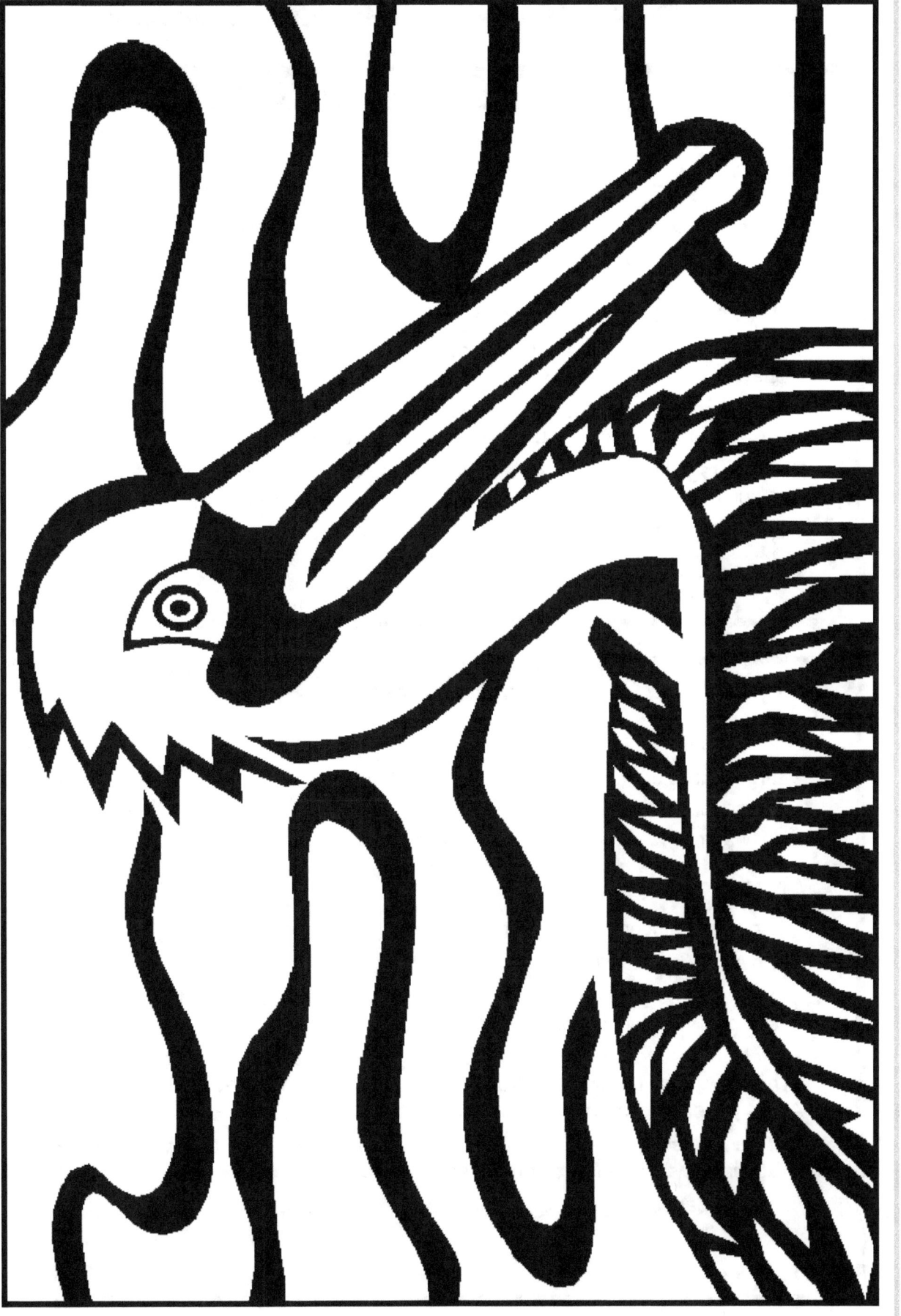

ELEMENTS OF DESIGN: FORM

Activity 1: Sand Sculpture Dough

What you need:
- 4 cups clean sand (not beach sand)
- 2 cups cornstarch
- 2 cups water
- Plastic utensils for carving

What to do:
1. Mix all ingredients in a saucepan.
2. Heat the mixture over medium heat and stir until it becomes as thick as modeling clay.
3. Once the mixture is the right consistency, allow it to cool before handling. **Note:** You may wish to make the dough beforehand and store it in an airtight container.
4. Encourage students to notice the interesting texture of the dough as they mold or "sculpt" it into various forms.
5. Allow the completed forms to air dry.

Activity 2: Paper-Mache Sculpture

What you need:
- Large plastic bowl
- Newsprint
- Hot water
- Plastic bag
- Flour
- Water
- Tempera paint
- Paintbrushes

What to do:
1. First have students tear enough small squares of newsprint to fill a large plastic bowl.
2. Cover the scraps with hot water and soak them overnight.
3. Demonstrate for students how to squeeze out the excess water from the newsprint scraps. Place the scraps into a plastic bag.
4. Make a paste of flour and water. Use 1/3 cup flour for every 1/4 cup water. Combine the paste with the newspaper scraps, using 1 cup of paste for every 3 cups of paper. Knead this paper-mache clay in the plastic bag.
5. When the consistency of the clay is good for molding, encourage students to form animals, insects, flowers or other small objects.
6. Let the paper-mache sculptures air dry and then paint them.

ELEMENTS OF DESIGN: FORM

Activity 3: Drawing People

What you need:

- White paper • Pencil and eraser • Coloring materials

What to do:

1. Demonstrate for students how the human body may be looked upon as a series of connected oval or sausage-like shapes.
2. Use a student as a model to draw, and help students see the breakdown of the oval body parts.
3. Once you have drawn all of the oval segments of the human form, erase the overlapping lines where body parts connect. Point out to students that there are joints where many body parts connect. Joints include the shoulders, knees and wrists.
4. Next, add clothing and other features to complete the drawing. Show students how to add lines to the area around joints to show bent limbs and creases.
5. Students are now ready to draw their humans. Have students work in pairs, so that they can be models for each other. Encourage students to draw their partner in various positions.

Activity 4: Animated People

What you need:

- White paper • Pencil and eraser • Coloring materials

What to do:

1. Review with students how the human body may be looked upon as a series of connected oval or sausage-like shapes.
2. Next, have students work in pairs. One partner will pose while the other partner will draw the partner in a series of 3–5 positions that show action, such as when participating in a sport.
3. Encourage students to draw details on their animated person and facial expressions.
4. Students should also add a background to their picture.

SYMMETRICAL DRAWINGS

Draw the other half of the picture using the grid as a guide. Color the picture.

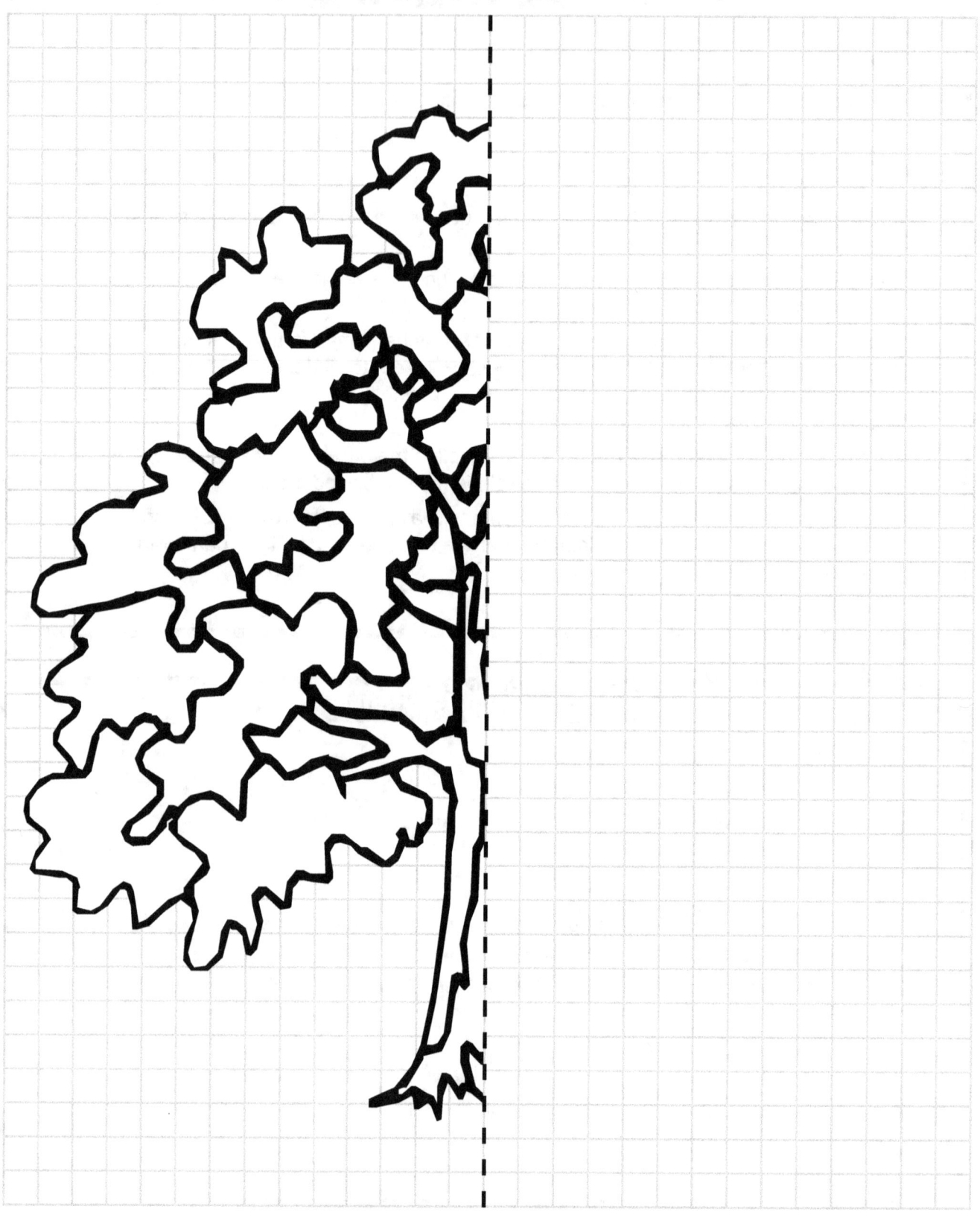

SYMMETRICAL DRAWINGS

Draw the other half of the picture using the grid as a guide. Color the picture.

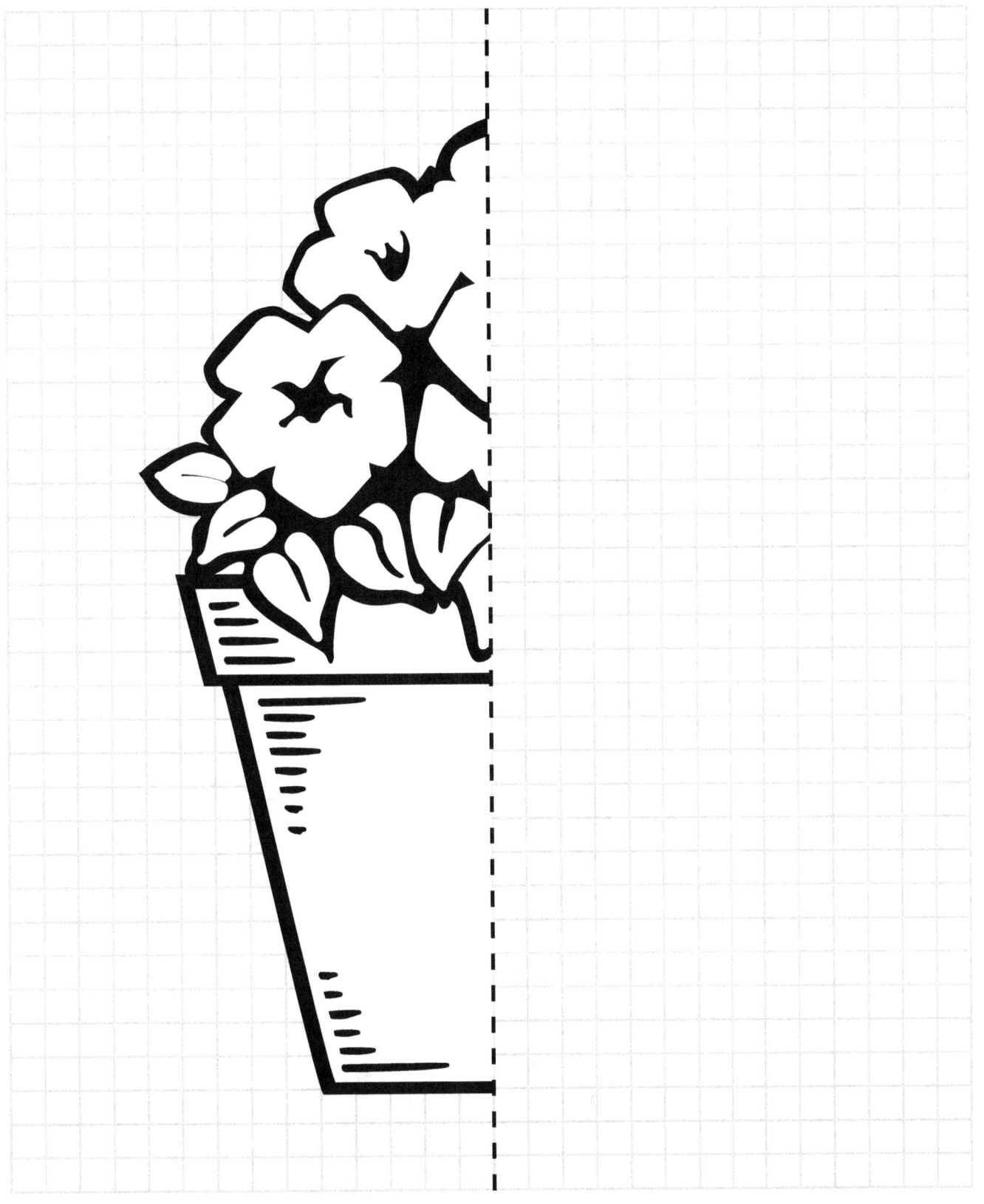

35

SYMMETRICAL DRAWINGS

Draw the other half of the picture using the grid as a guide. Color the picture.

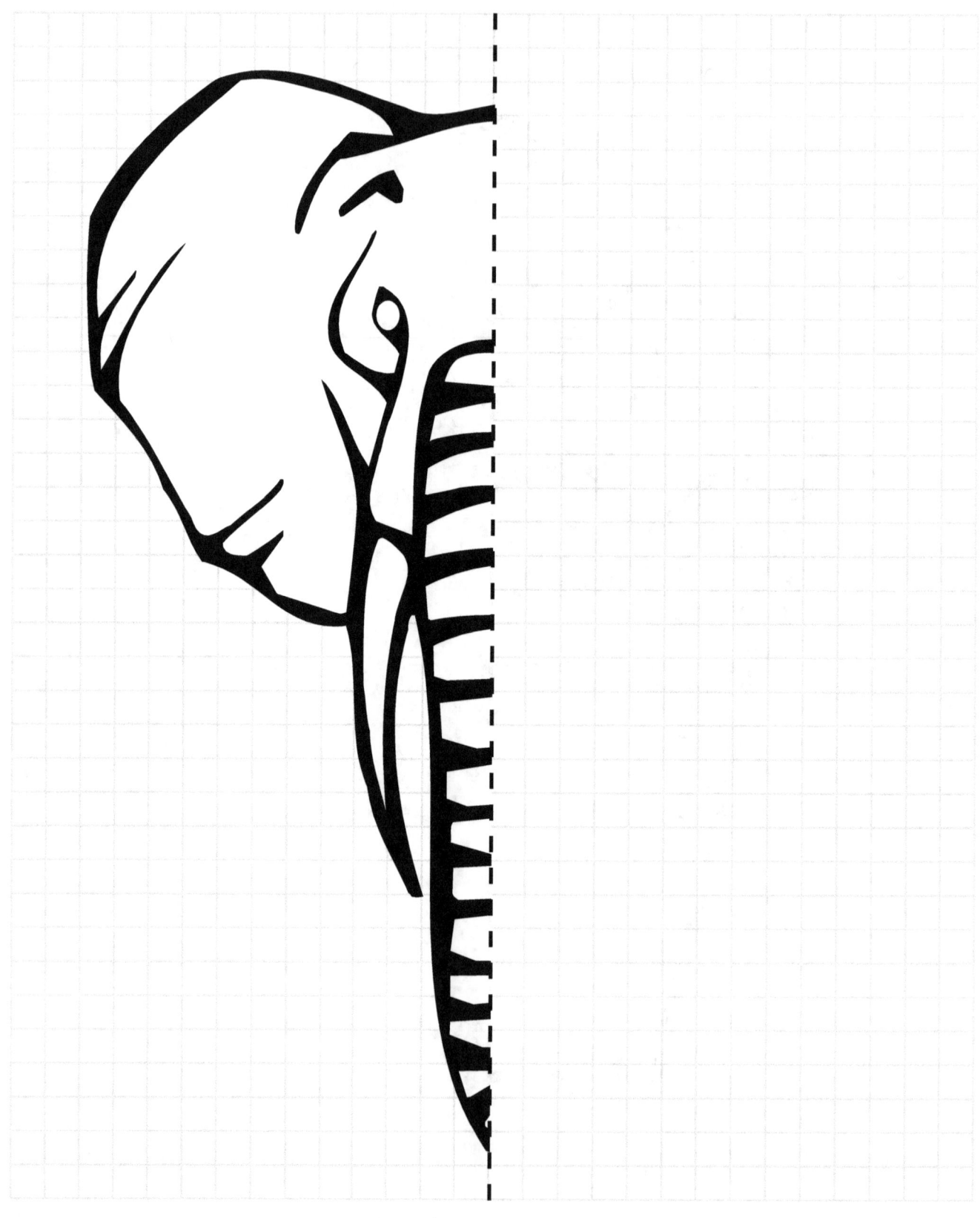

SYMMETRY CUTOUT

Cut out a face from a magazine. Cut it in half and glue one half below. Draw and color the other half of the face.

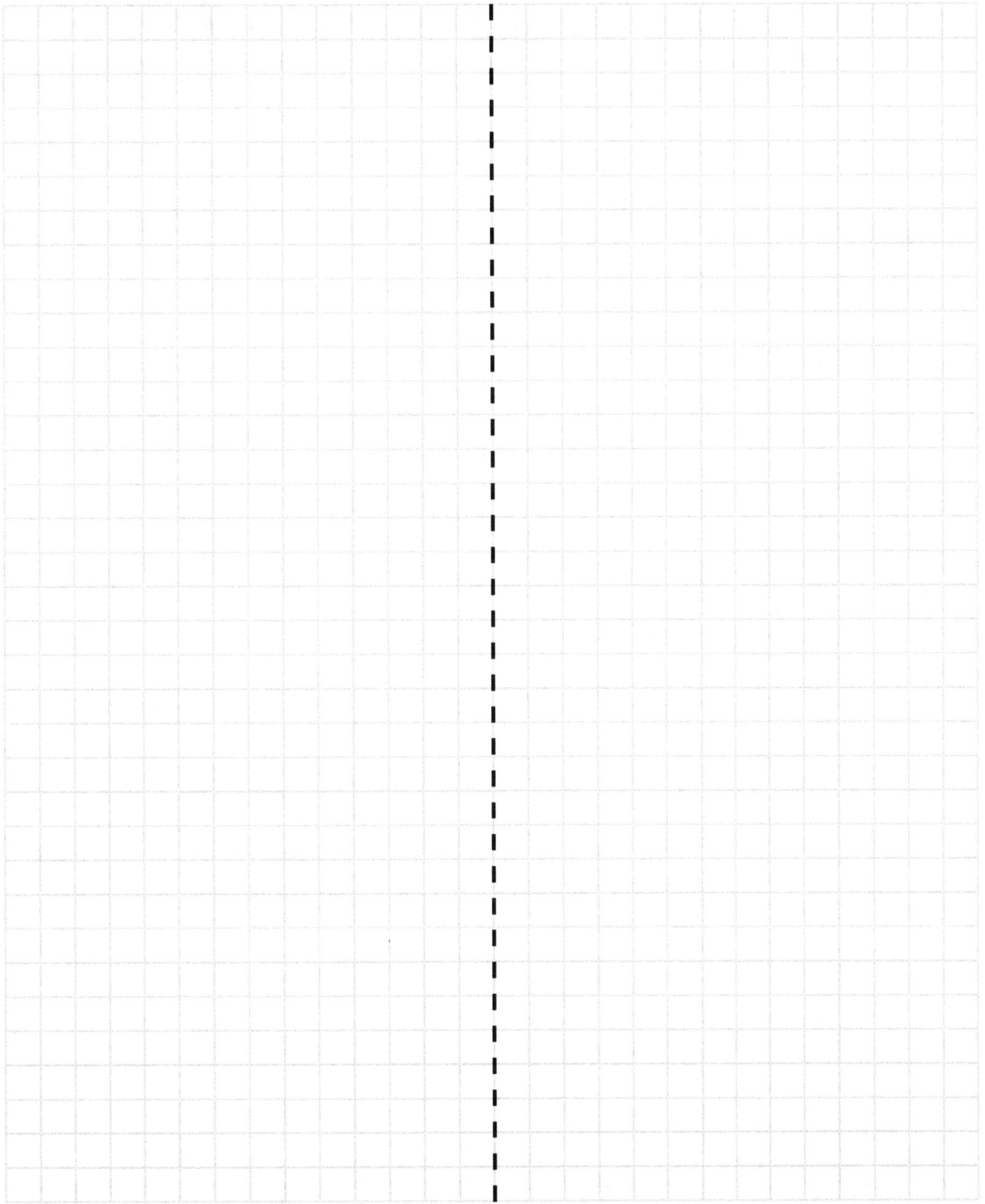

AMERICAN VETERAN MEMORIAL

Allegory: The use of symbolic figures to represent abstract ideas such as honor and sacrifice.

Design an American Veteran memorial. Think about the symbols that you would like to incorporate into your design and explain your thinking on a separate piece of paper.

CREATE A STAMP

Create a stamp.

Write about your stamp:

_____

_____

_____

FANTASY CREATURE FILL-IN

Use these body parts to draw your own fantasy creature.

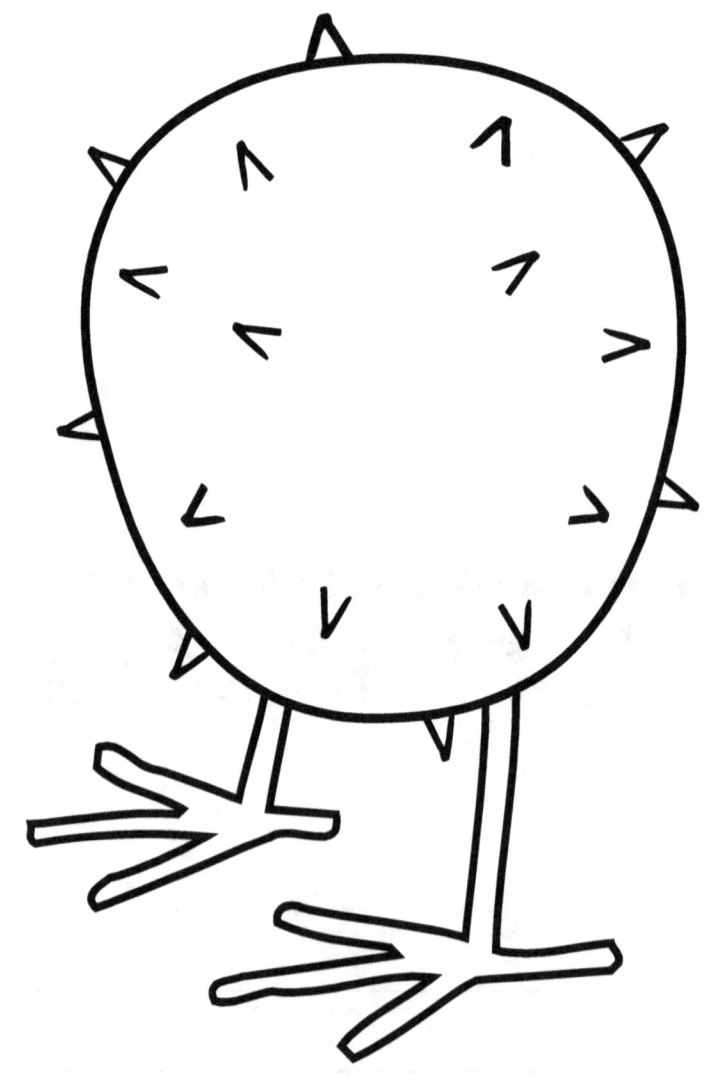

FANTASY CREATURE FILL-IN

Use these body parts to draw your own fantasy creature.

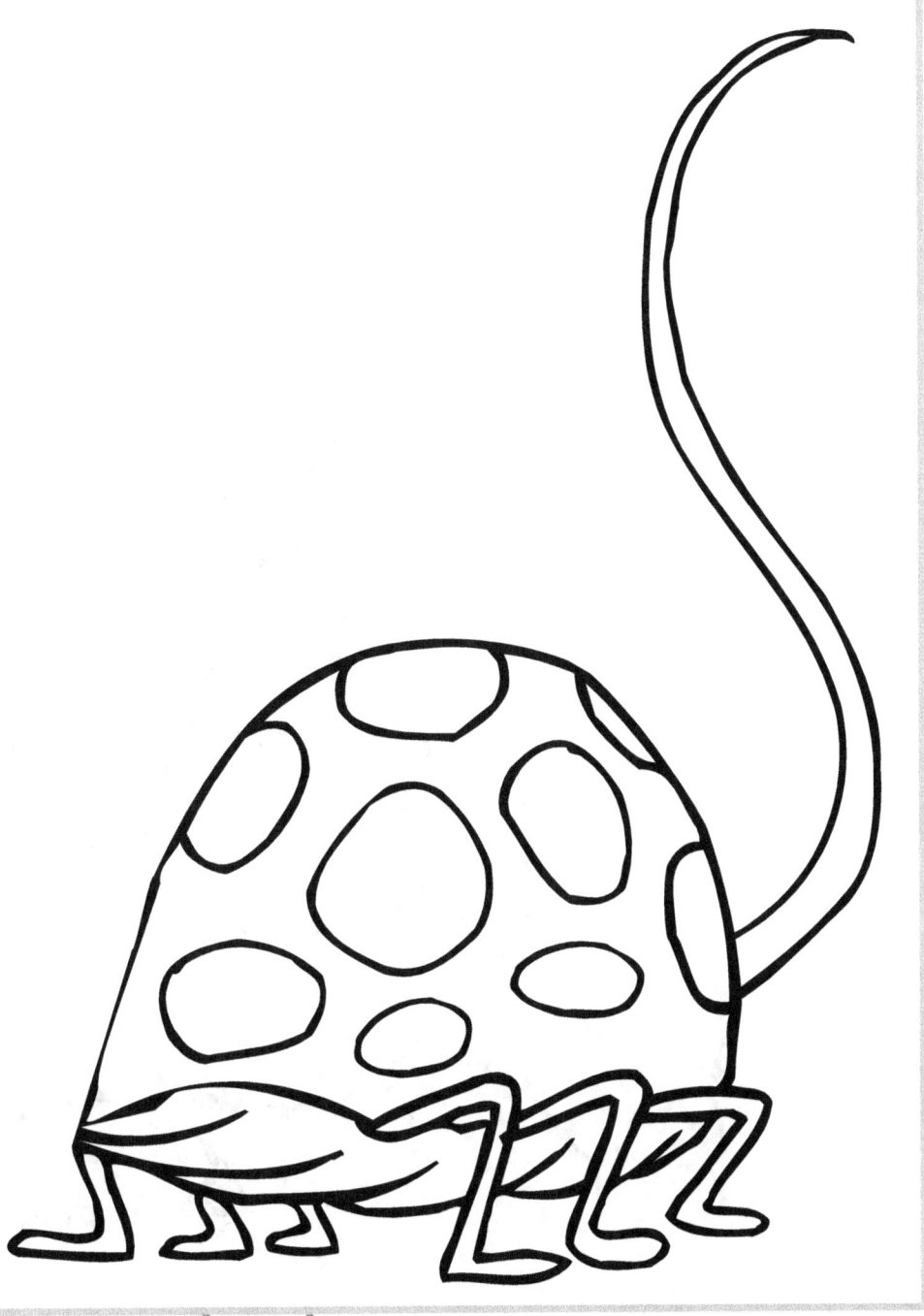

FANTASY CREATURE FILL-IN

Use these body parts to draw your own fantasy creature.

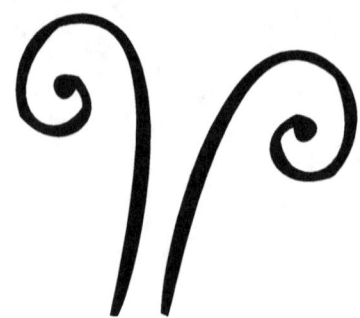

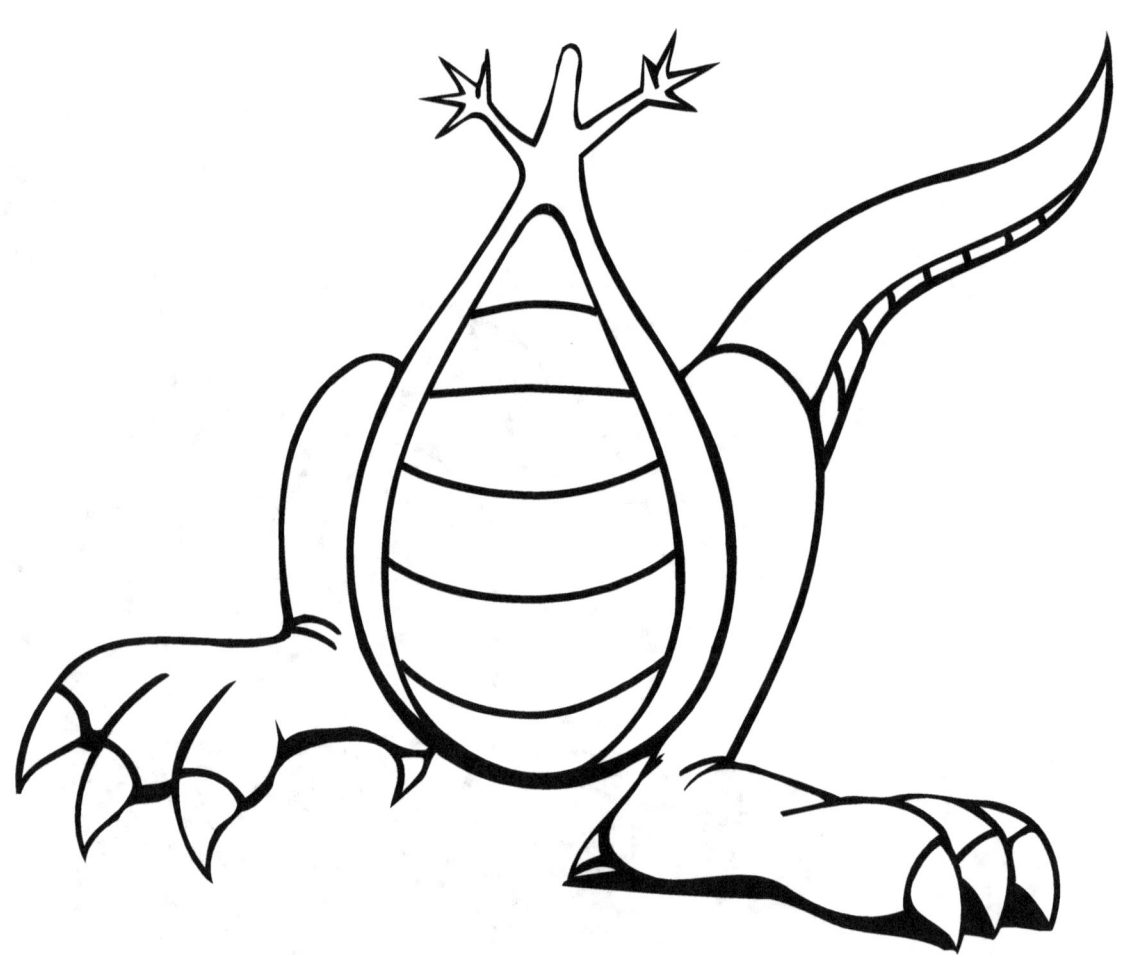

ELEMENTS OF DESIGN: TEXTURE

Activity 1: Sandpaper Designs

What you need:
- Sandpaper • Crayons • Iron • Paper

What to do:
1. Invite students to color a design or picture on sandpaper. They should press heavily into the paper as they color, to deposit a lot of wax onto the sandpaper.
2. Next, demonstrate for students how to carefully lay paper on top of their picture and run a warm iron over the paper. Show students how the heat will transfer a gravel-like print of their picture onto the paper.
3. After students have made one print, they can color their design or picture using a different color scheme and make a second print

Activity 2: Texture Mania

What you need:
- Large piece of paper
- Glue
- Black markers
- Paint
- Various materials such as sawdust, torn construction paper, tissue paper, crushed eggshells, newsprint, etc.
- Paintbrushes

What to do:
1. Instruct students to draw an outline picture on their paper using a black marker.
2. Then, have students glue on different materials to fill in the different sections of the drawing.
3. Once the materials have dried and all of the sections of the drawing have been filled, encourage students to add paint to their artwork.

EXPERIMENT WITH TEXTURE

Encourage students to create different textures with the tools, materials, and papers listed below. They can use the textures to create a collage or to fill sections of a picture.

Out-of-the-Ordinary Painting Tools

- Fingers
- Sticks
- Blocks of wood
- Branches
- Rope
- Feathers
- Leaves
- Sponges
- Tissues
- Brushes
- Cotton swabs
- Cotton balls
- Plastic pot scrubbers
- Plastic wrap
- Makeup brushes

Excellent Drawing and Painting Materials

- Crayons
- Pencils
- Pastels
- Chalk
- Charcoal
- Ink pen
- Water-based markers
- Acrylic paint
- Makeup
- Tempera paint
- Felt tip pens
- Pencil crayons
- Watercolors
- Food coloring

A Variety of Surfaces on Which to Paint or Draw

- Newsprint
- Paper plates
- Blocks of wood
- Tissue paper
- Paper bags
- Sandpaper
- Wet paper
- Cardboard
- Fabric
- Plastic wrap
- Paper towels
- Waxed paper
- Aluminum foil
- Stones
- Foam

CREATE DIFFERENT TEXTURES

Corn Syrup Paint

Make a striking paint with an interesting texture by combining food coloring and light corn syrup. Mix up as many colors as needed. Encourage students to paint different landscapes or oceanscapes. Students may wish to first create an outline drawing with a permanent marker before painting. Be sure to allow more than a day of drying time.

Flour-and-Water Finger Paint

This paint will help you to achieve great textures when finger painting. Mix 1 cup flour, 1 cup water and 2 teaspoons salt in a small container to make a paint with the consistency of thick gravy. Add in the desired food coloring. Repeat the process for as many colors as needed.

Glossy Paint

Give tempera paint a wet, glossy look by combining 1 part white glue and 1 part tempera paint.

Puff Paint

Have students create unique pictures using puff paint. Combine 1 cup salt, 1 cup sugar and the desired food coloring in a squeeze bottle. Shake the ingredients and squeeze the paint out of the bottle onto the paper.

Sand Paint

Sand paint offers an interesting option when striving to create texture in a picture. Begin by having students create a simple outline drawing. Then make the sand paint by combining 1 part sand and 5 parts powdered tempera. Encourage students to experiment when mixing the sand and tempera to achieve the desired color. Next, when a few sand paint colors have been made, use a wooden craft stick to spread a thin layer of glue in one section of the outline drawing. Then, using a spoon, gently pour the sand paint into the glue-covered section. Lightly lift the paper to shake off any excess sand paint. Allow the sand painting to dry, and seal it using hair spray.

Wax Resist

As wax and water don't mix, the wax resist technique can be used to mask out areas to preserve the white of the paper or the color beneath and to create appealing textures. Draw or color with a wax crayon and then wash over it with a water-based paint.

MAKING TEXTURED PAPER

What you need:

- Large tub
- Assorted papers
- Cornstarch
- Books
- Blender
- Wax paper
- Rolling pin
- Warm water
- Measuring spoons
- Materials that add color and texture (e.g., glitter, food coloring, seeds)
- Materials with which to imprint the paper (e.g., plants, lace, buttons)

What to do:

1. Tear the assorted papers into tiny bits and pieces. Students can separate the papers by color.
2. Soak the torn paper in a tub of warm water for at least a few hours.
3. Add torn paper and water to a blender. Use 1 cup paper for every 2–3 cups water. Blend the mixture on medium-high until it is creamy and smooth, to make a pulp.
4. Add 1 tablespoon of cornstarch, to make the resulting paper less porous to ink and paper. Students can also add food coloring, glitter, or tiny materials that will create texture in their papers (e.g., seeds). Blend the mixture for about 10 seconds after each addition.
5. Lay a large piece of wax paper on a table.
6. Measure out about half a cup of pulp and squeeze out excess water by hand. Smooth the pulp out onto the wax paper in a thin layer.
7. Students can press plants, lace, or other textured materials into the pulp, to create imprints.
8. Lay a second piece of wax paper over the thin layer of pulp and use a rolling pin to roll out any excess water.
9. Repeat the above process to make layers of new and different papers.
10. Weigh down all the new papers with books and allow them to dry.
11. When the papers are dry, carefully peel away the layers of wax paper.

TEXTURE HUNT

Find examples of different textures and reproduce them by making rubbings on this page.

LANDSCAPE ART

Lay the landscape on different surfaces (such as sandpaper) while you color it. This will produce a variety of textures.

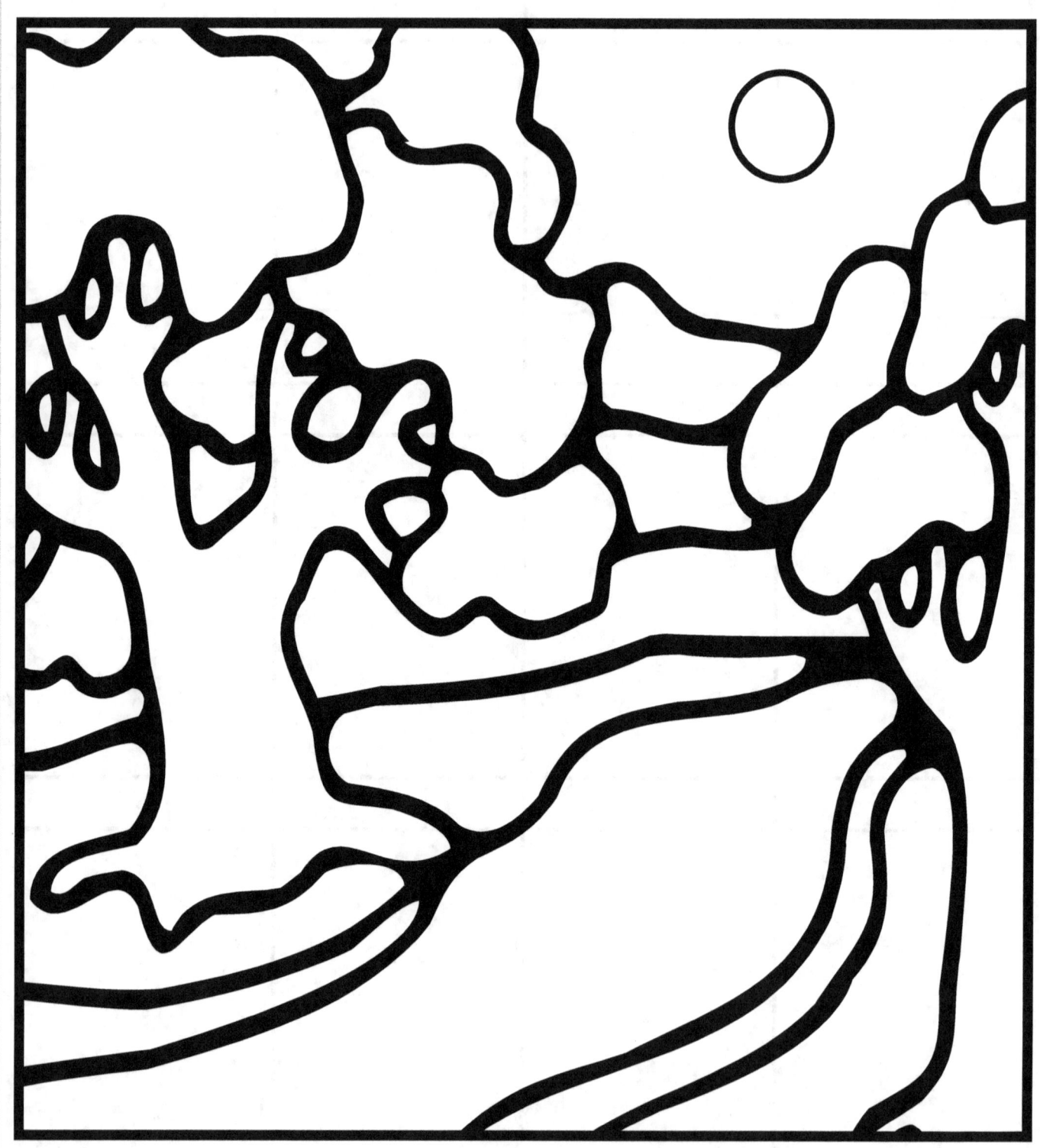

LANDSCAPE ART

Paint the landscape using watercolors.

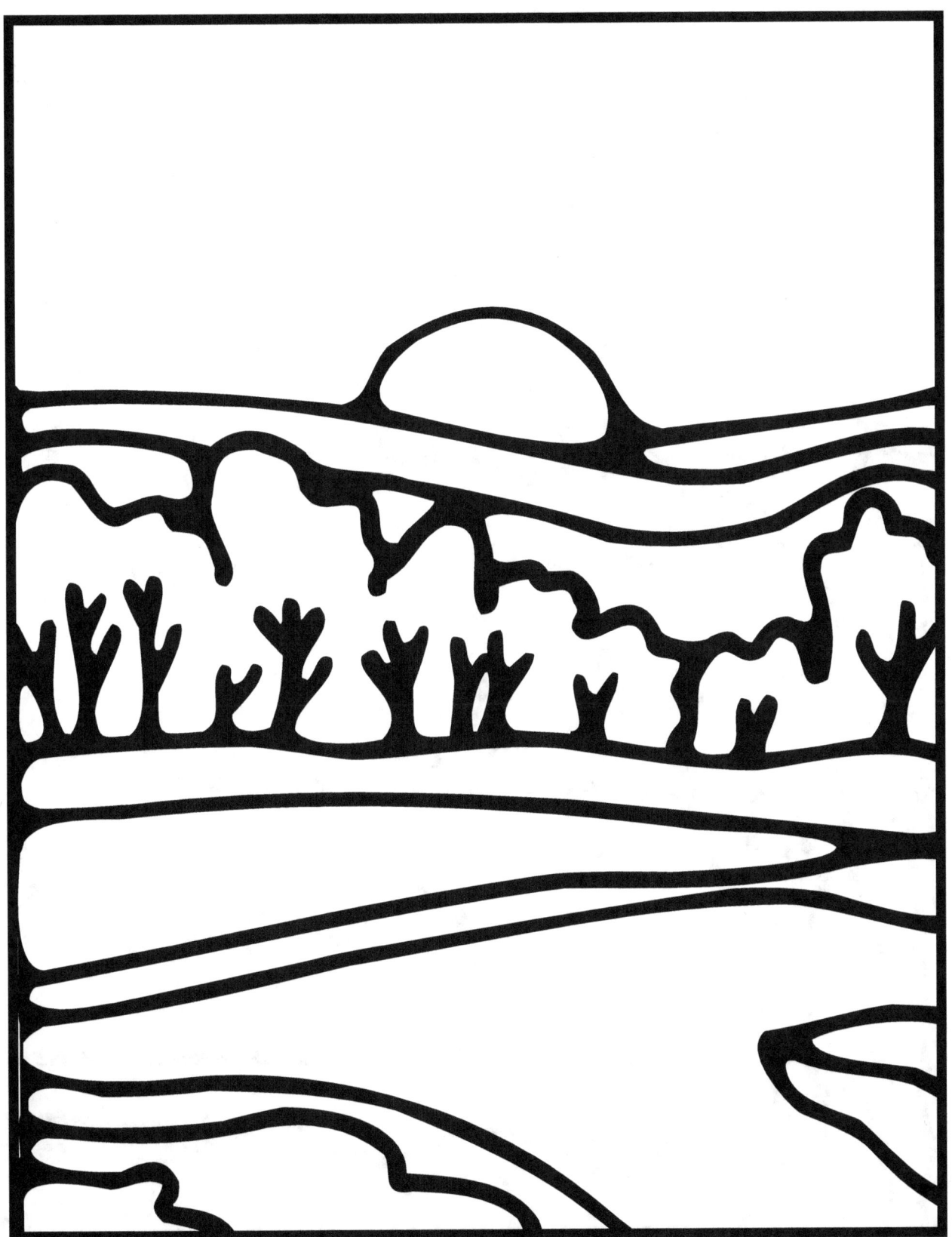

LANDSCAPE ART

Fill in sections of the landscape using different colors of Plasticine.

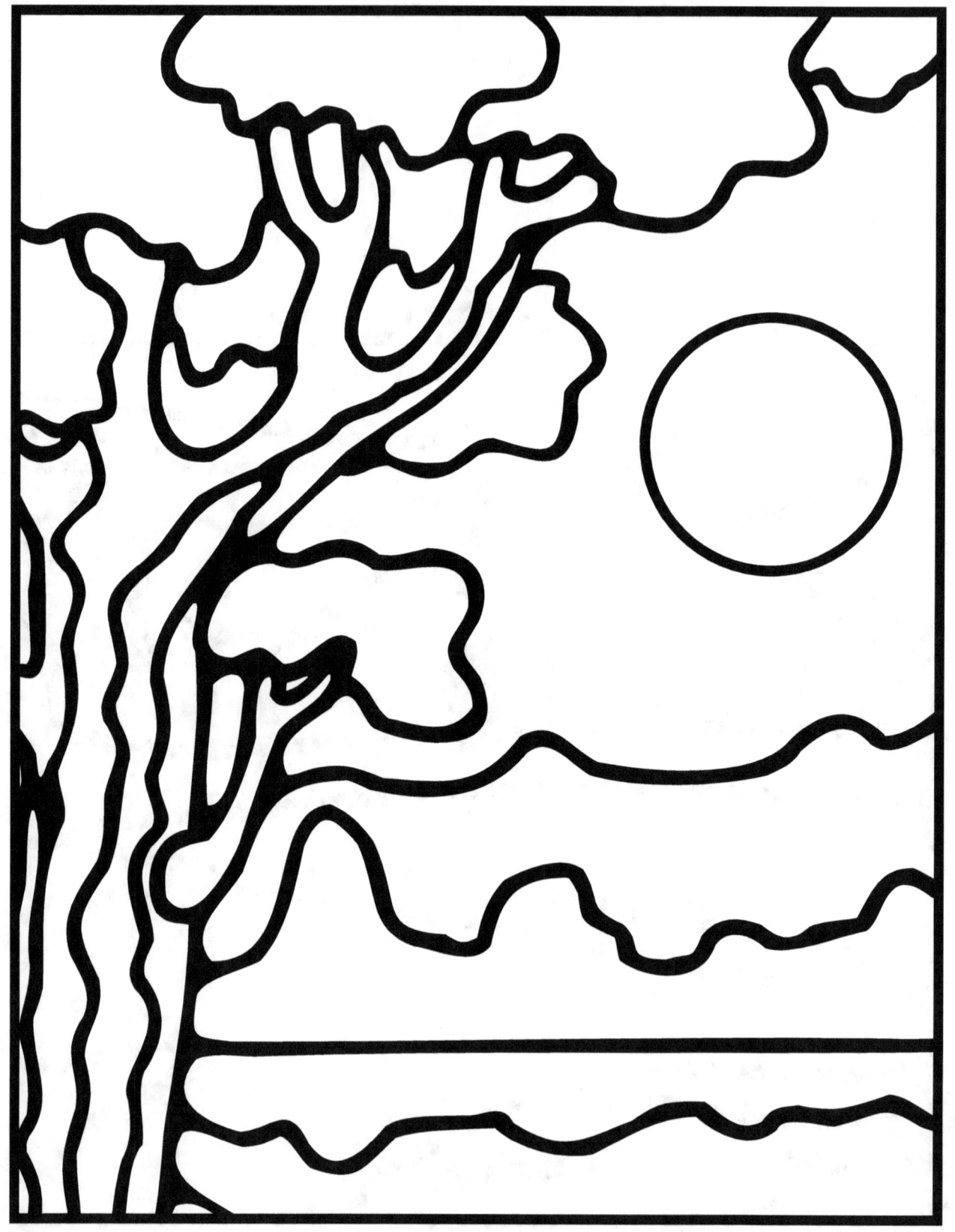

50

LANDSCAPE ART

Color the landscape using oil pastels and set it with hair spray.

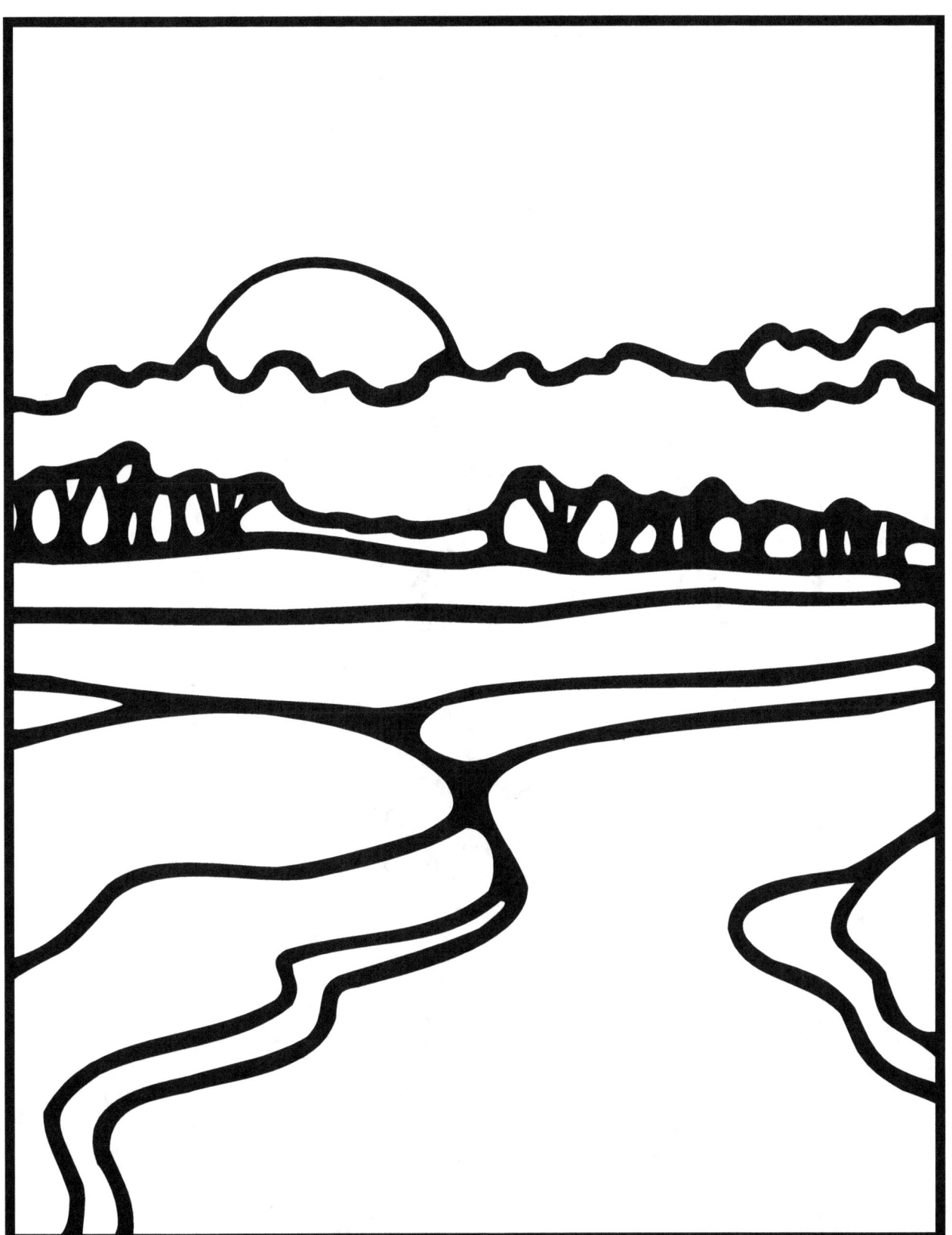

SPORTS FUN

Fill in the sections of the picture using torn bits of construction paper.

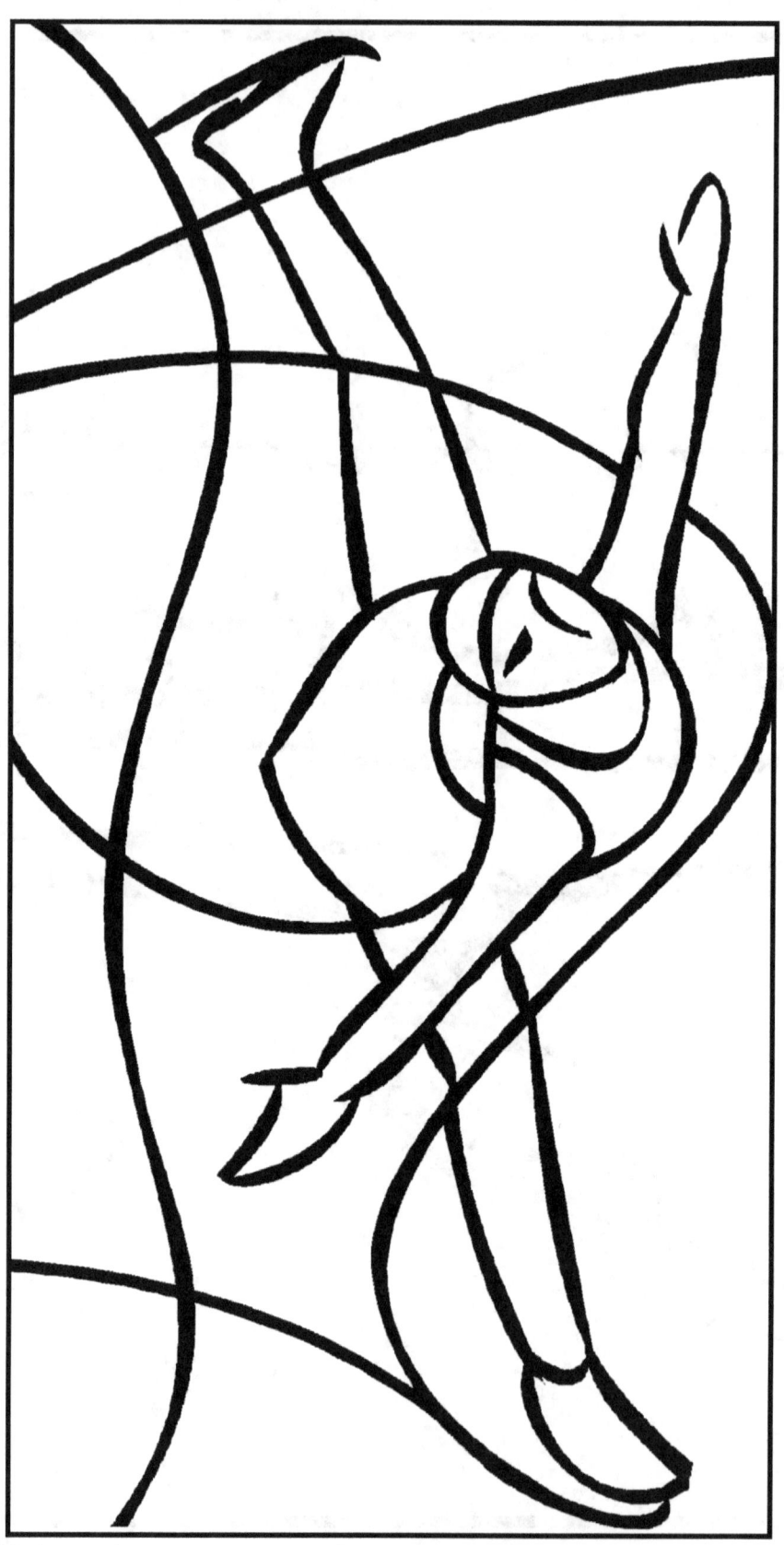

ELEMENTS OF DESIGN: SPACE

Activity 1: Landscape

What you need:
- White paper
- Oil pastels
- Cotton balls for smudging

What to do:

1. Review with students the art terms foreground, middle ground and background and tell them that they will be painting a landscape. Look at and discuss examples of landscapes.
2. To begin, show students how to lightly sketch with their pencil these three sections using ground, water and ground.
3. Instruct students to fill each section with paint. Encourage students to mix colors and to use more than one shade or tint of color.
4. Once the sections are completely covered with paint, have students add details and objects to the sections using darker colors. Remind students that objects in the foreground are the most prominent and appear to be the closest to the viewer. Alternatively, objects that are smaller are intended to appear farther away from the viewer.

Activity 2: Streetscape in One-Point Perspective

What you need:
- Coloring materials
- Pencil
- Eraser
- Ruler

What to do:

1. Review with students the art terms perspective, horizon line and vanishing point. Show examples of each term and how they are used in artwork.
2. Explain to students that they will draw a streetscape in one-point perspective. Have students begin by drawing a horizon line on their papers.
3. Next, students should find the midpoint of the horizon line and mark it as the vanishing point for their drawing.
4. Demonstrate for students how to mark the bottom right and left corners of their paper and then draw a line from each mark to the vanishing point. This will create the illusion of a street.
5. Have students add three-dimensional buildings along each side of the street. Remind students that buildings should decrease in size as they approach the vanishing point.
6. Encourage students to add other details to their drawings, along both the street and the horizon line.

ELEMENTS OF DESIGN: SPACE

Activity 3: Light, Shade and Shadow

What you need:
- Black construction paper
- White construction paper
- Bristol board
- Pencil
- Eraser
- Glue
- Masking tape

What to do:

1. Tape a large piece of white construction paper onto a wall in a room with dim lighting.
2. One student holds the flashlight so that it shines onto the white construction paper. Another student sits between the light and the paper so that the shadow of their profile appears on the paper. A third student traces the outline of the second student's profile onto the paper.
3. Repeat steps 1 and 2 until each student has a copy of their profile.
4. Instruct students to cut their profile out of the white paper, place it onto three pieces of black construction paper, trace around it, and cut out the resulting three black silhouettes.
5. Students glue the black silhouettes onto white construction paper to create a series of shadows.

Activity 4: Positive and Negative Shapes

What you need:
- Squares of construction paper (black and colored)
- Scissors
- Glue

What to do:

1. Discuss with students the concept of positive and negative spaces in artwork.
2. Instruct students to trace one or more geometric shapes onto one square of black construction paper and one square of colored construction paper.
3. Have students cut out the geometric shapes.
4. Next, have students glue the black geometric shapes onto colored construction paper and the colored geometric shapes onto black construction paper.

THINKING ABOUT SPACE

Color the picture. **BRAIN STRETCH:** How is the element of space used in this picture?

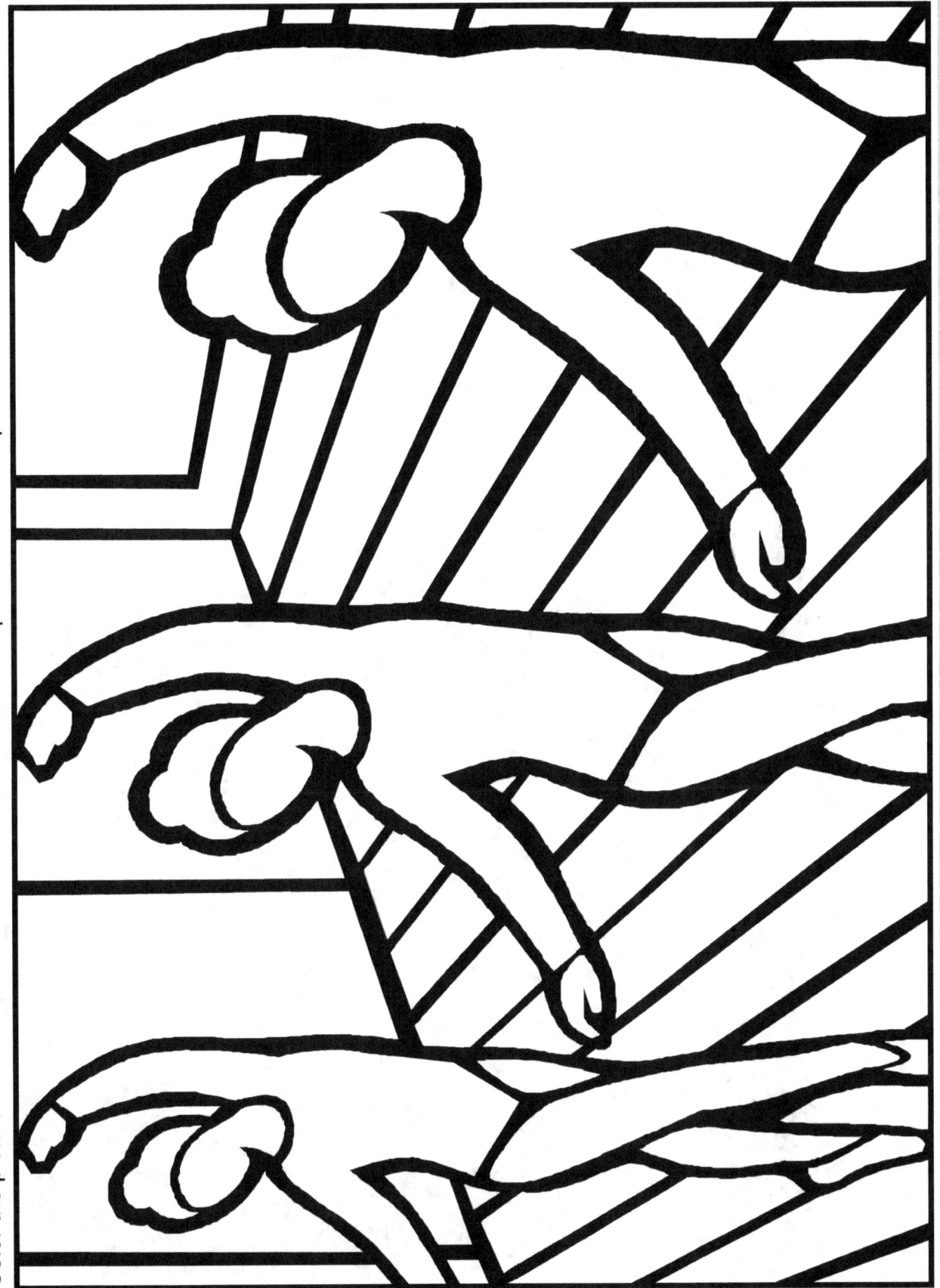

ONE-POINT PERSPECTIVE

Complete the picture by adding a horizon line and vanishing point. Add details to the picture and color.

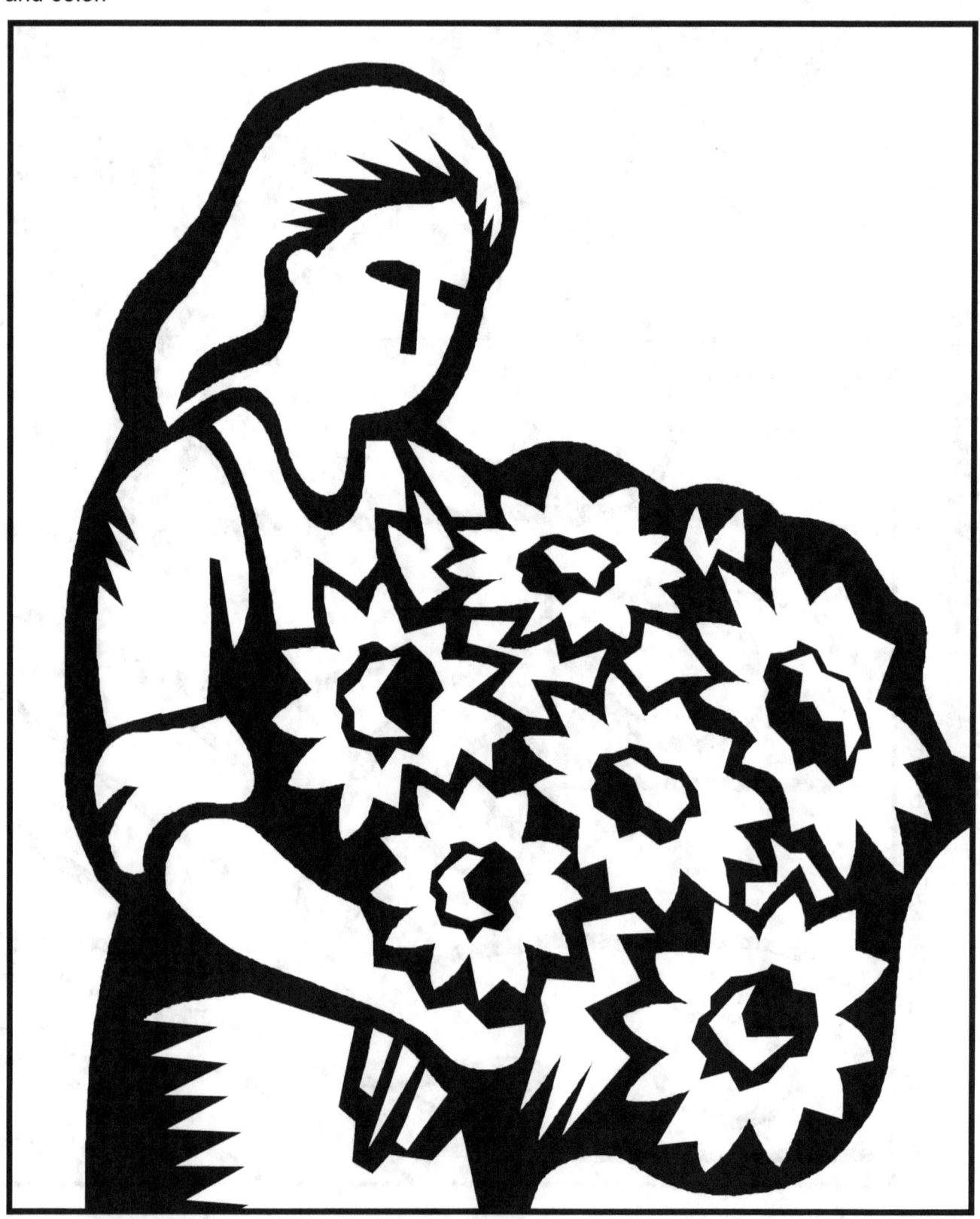

WORKING WITH ELEMENTS OF DESIGN

Complete the picture using different elements of design. On a separate piece of paper, explain how you used the elements.

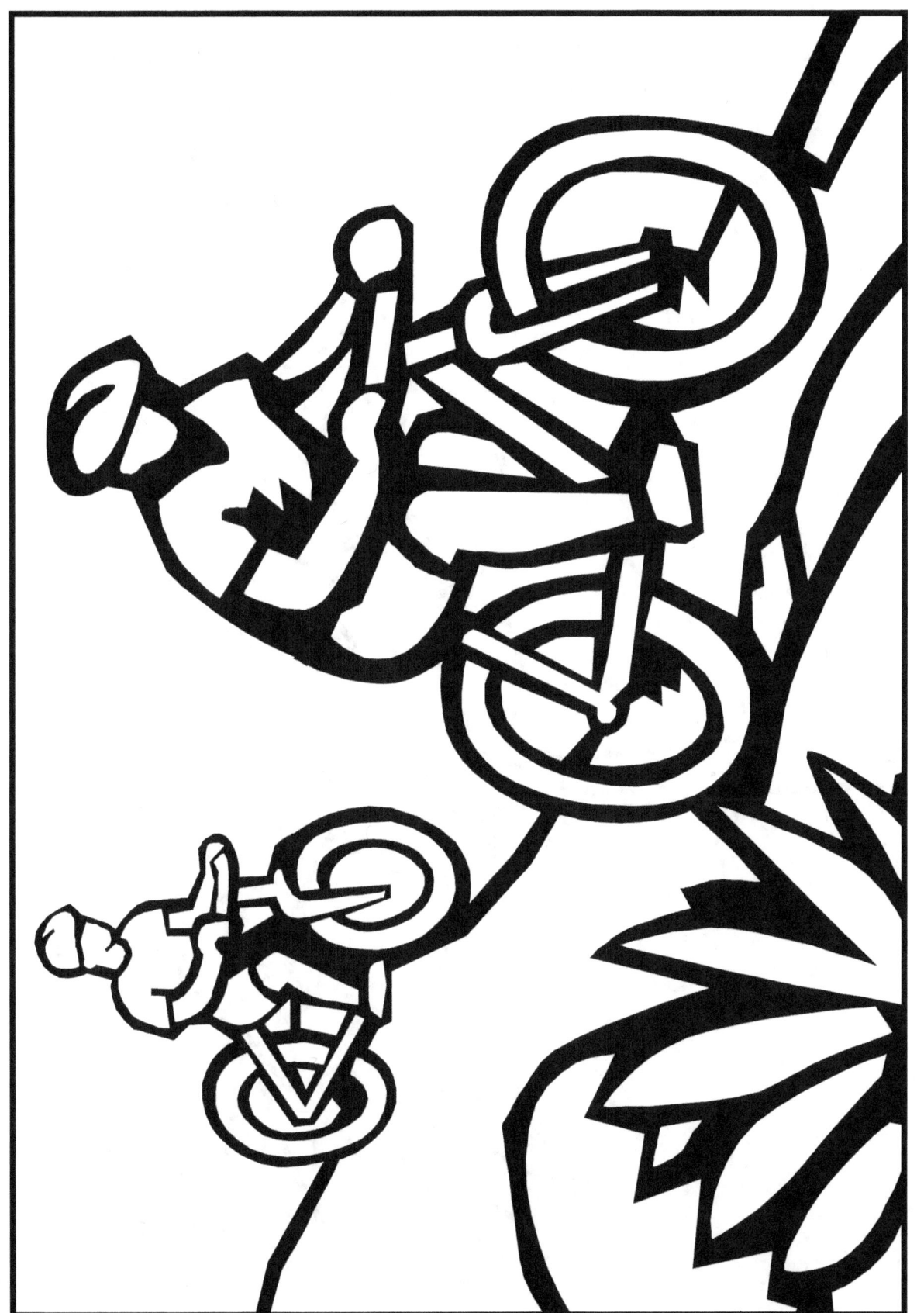

WORKING WITH ELEMENTS OF DESIGN

Complete the picture using different elements of design. On a separate piece of paper, explain how you used the elements.

CUTOUT ART

Create a picture using images cut out of old magazines.

WORKING WITH ELEMENTS OF DESIGN

Add a logo to the hockey player's uniform. Think about elements of design and add other details to the picture. Explain what you did on a separate piece of paper.

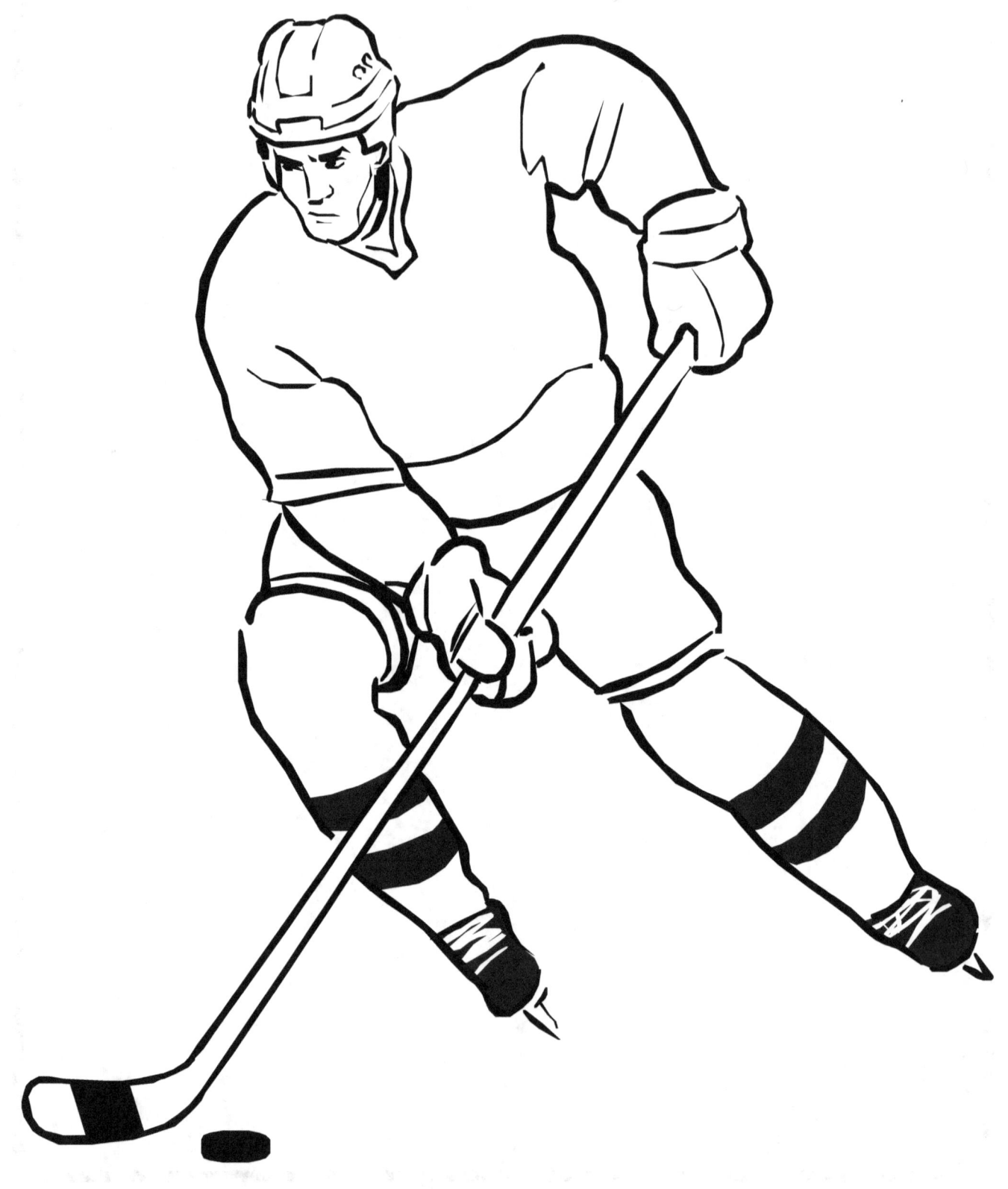

WORKING WITH ELEMENTS OF DESIGN

Use elements of design to color the picture. Explain what you did on a separate piece of paper.

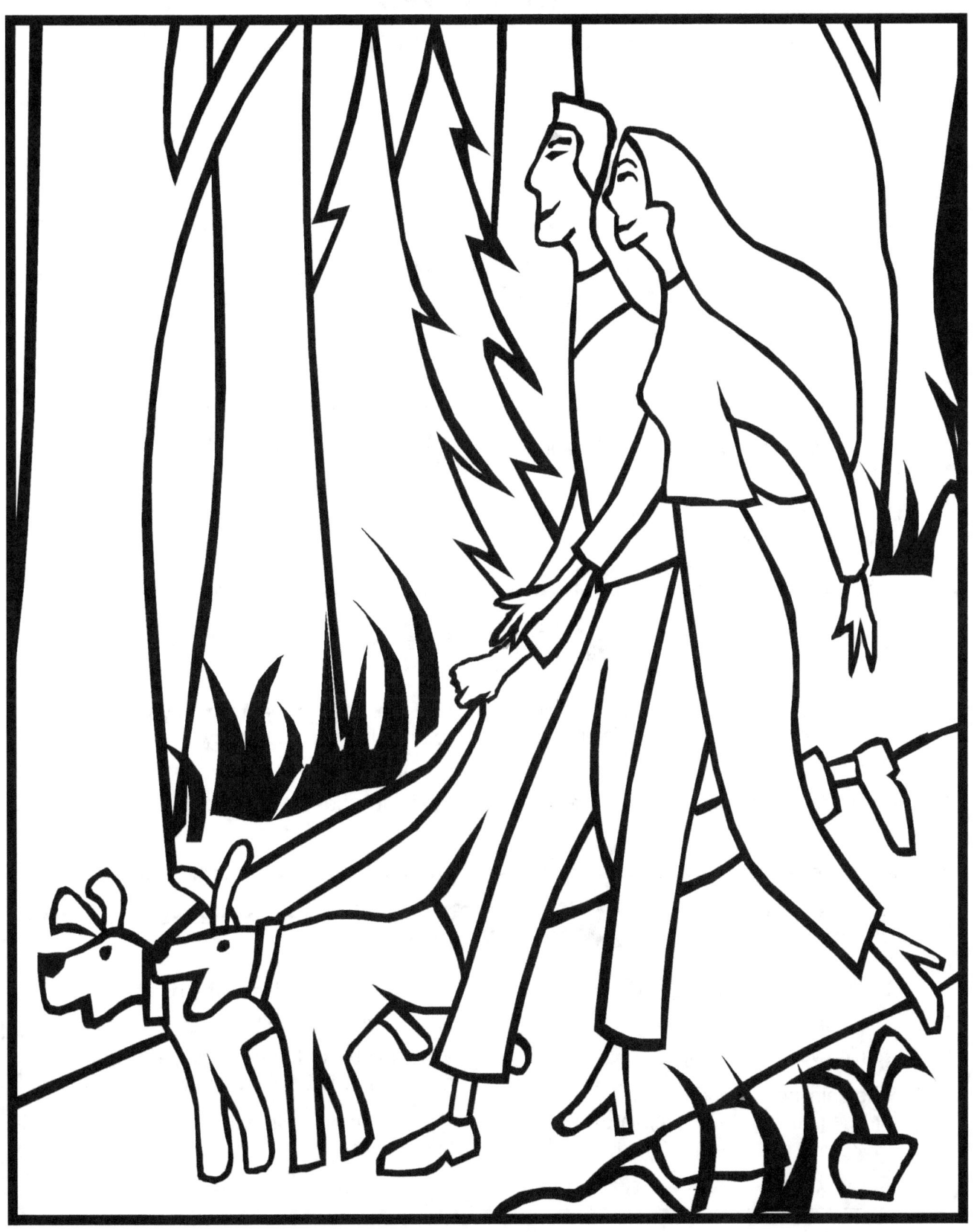

ART DISCUSSION PROMPTS: LOOKING AT A PAINTING

Description

- Describe the subject of the painting.
- What colors do you see?
- What shapes do you see?
- What textures do you see?
- What kind of lines do you see?
- What kind of objects do you see?
- What kind of forms do you see?

Analysis

- What is the focal point of the painting?
- Is there an element of design that is most prominent in the painting? Explain.
- Do you think the composition is balanced? Explain.
- Does the artist show movement in the painting? If so, how?
- Does the painting have a sense of three dimensions?
- What angle of view do you think the artist had when painting this subject? Explain your thinking.

Interpretation

- What kind of mood do you think the artist is trying to encourage when viewing the painting?
- How does the painting make you feel?
- What message or meaning do you think the artist is trying to convey?
- Why do you think the artist chose to paint this particular subject?

Personal Opinion

- Do you like the painting? Why or why not?
- What, if anything, does this painting remind you of? Explain.
- The painting is a good example of … or The painting is a bad example of …
- Do you think the title of the painting is a good one? Explain.
- Would you like to see more paintings from this artist? Why or why not?
- Would you buy this painting? Why or why not?

ARTIST-INSPIRED ART IDEAS

Artist: Theodore Dragonieri

Theodore Dragonieri is a Canadian artist who fixes old shoes, then paints and collages them in the styles of famous artists.

What you need:

- Pictures of Theodore Dragonieri's painted shoes
- Pairs of old shoes
- Paintbrushes
- Acrylic or tempera paints with white glue added to them
- Paper and pencils
- Water and containers

What to do:

1. Display pictures of Theodore Dragonieri's shoe art and discuss it as a class. Ask students what they think of it.
2. Ask students to think about artists they like. Have them choose one of the artists.
3. Have students sketch a drawing that they will paint onto the shoes.
4. Distribute materials and have students remove any laces from the shoes.
5. When students have finalized their design, have them paint it onto the shoes. To make dark shoes easier to paint on, students may first prime them with white paint.
6. When the shoes are finished, have classmates try to guess which artist each student was inspired by.

Artist: Randy McGovern

Randy McGovern is one of the best-known wildlife artists in America. His paintings are extremely detailed, and most paintings contain several hidden small animals.

What you need:

- Wildlife photos (calendars are usually an excellent source) • Coloring pencils • Paper

What to do:

1. Display for students examples of Randy McGovern's art and discuss it as a class. Ask students what they think of the paintings.
2. Pass around the examples and have students look closely at the way the artist painted fur and feathers on the animals. Draw attention to the short brushstrokes and the different colors placed side by side.
3. Have students choose a wildlife photograph to draw.
4. Ask students to draw a simple pencil sketch of their chosen animal. Students should then add color and details to make their drawing look realistic.
5. Encourage students to take their time and to think about shading, line and colors.
6. When students are finished, invite them to share their drawings with the class.

ARTIST-INSPIRED ART IDEAS

Artist: Andy Warhol

Andy Warhol was a leader in the pop art movement. He created bright-colored images of everyday objects such as soup cans and comics, and of famous people such as musicians and movie stars. His paintings were meant to show that art was for everybody.

What you need:

- Examples of Andy Warhol's paintings
- White drawing paper
- Assorted markers or tempera paints
- Pencils

What to do:

1. Display for students examples of Andy Warhol's paintings and discuss them as a class.
2. With students, brainstorm a list of well-known brands of soda, clothing, running shoes, restaurants, toys, games, television characters, comic book characters, and more.
3. Distribute the materials.
4. Model folding a sheet of white drawing paper into quarters. Have students fold their own sheet of paper the same way.
5. Model drawing identical pictures of one of the branded items in all four boxes. Use different colors of paint or markers to finish each of the drawings.
6. Have students create and color their own drawings in the same manner.

Artist: Vincent van Gogh

Vincent van Gogh was a self-taught artist and is one of the best-known painters from the 19th century. Van Gogh painted scenes and objects from everyday life the way he saw them, capturing light and shadow, textures, movement, and vivid colors.

What you need:

- Picture of Vincent van Gogh's painting *Starry Night*
- White drawing paper
- Tempera paints
- Paintbrushes

What to do:

1. On Day 1, display for students Van Gogh's painting *Starry Night*. Discuss the painting as a class.
2. Draw students' attention to Van Gogh's depiction of the wind. Discuss as a class the many shades of blue paint and the swirled brushstrokes.
3. Distribute materials, then model how to paint in Van Gogh's style. Paint dark-blue swirls on the top two-thirds of the paper. Have students paint swirls on their paper.
4. Model painting the rest of the sky white. Point out that you are allowing the paint to mix on the paper, the way Van Gogh did. Have students paint the sky in the same manner.
5. Model making short brushstrokes over the swirls to give the impression of movement. Have students make short brushstrokes on their paintings.
6. Choose another of Van Gogh's painting, and ask students to identify the same painting techniques (swirls, the mixing of colors, and short brushstrokes).
7. On Day 2, ask students what they see at the bottom of *Starry Night*. Model how to paint the mountains and the town. Have students paint the town and mountains.

ARTIST-INSPIRED ART IDEAS

Artist: Henri Rousseau

Henri Rousseau was a self-taught French painter who created fantasy paintings. He borrowed ideas for his paintings from photographs, engravings, catalogs, and paintings that were created by other people. From those sources, he could see the correct posture of people and animals and find good compositions for his paintings.

What you need:

- Examples of Henri Rousseau's jungle paintings
- Scrap paper
- Permanent black markers
- White drawing paper
- Oil pastels
- Watercolor paints
- Paintbrushes
- Containers for water

What to do:

1. On Day 1, display examples of Henri Rousseau's jungle paintings for students to view.
2. Point out and discuss the foreground, middle ground, and background in Rousseau's paintings. Model using horizon lines for the foreground, middle ground, and background.
3. Model drawing large, simple shapes to create grass, leaves, and flowers. Point out that repeating a color or an object such as a flower can help tie the parts of the painting together.
4. Distribute scrap paper and permanent black markers. Have students make a rough sketch of their jungle scene. Remind them to use large shapes. Encourage students to add a simple animal and a sun or moon to their drawing.
5. When students are finished, have them re-create their pictures on the white drawing paper with a permanent black marker.
6. On Day 2, model "painting" with oil pastels. Create shading and depth by layering and blending colors. Point out again that it is important to repeat colors.
7. Distribute oil pastels. Have students color the animal(s), tree(s), sun or moon, and the flowers and blades of grass in the foreground. **Note:** Students should not color the sky in the background or the grass or ground in the middle ground.
8. On Day 3, distribute watercolor paints, brushes, and containers of water.
9. Have students use the water and brush to wet the sky area. Students can use blue and purple watercolors to paint the sky.
10. Have students use clean water and a brush to wet the grass area. Students can use any combination of yellow, green, blue and brown to paint the grass or ground.

AN ARTIST'S LIFE

Create a timeline of the significant events in the life a famous artist. Use this graphic organizer to help you.

Name of artist: _____

I chose this famous artist because _____
_____
_____

DATE	EVENT

SIMILARITIES AND DIFFERENCES

Describe two artworks.

Artist and description of artwork	Artist and description of artwork

Compare

How are the artworks **similar**?

_____
_____
_____
_____

Contrast

How are the artworks **different**?

_____
_____
_____
_____

DIRECT DRAW

Encourage students to think of art as the personal interpretation of ideas. This quick activity demonstrates how students given the same directions will each produce a unique artwork. Collect and display all of the students' completed artworks. You will have a wonderful collection of abstract art based on shape, color and line.

WHAT YOU NEED:

- piece of square paper
- coloring materials

WHAT TO DO:

1. Tell students that they will each complete a piece of art by following your oral directions. Before you begin, ask students to predict whether or not all the students' works will look the same.

2. Give each student the same materials.

3. Call out directions. For example:
   - Draw a thin line across the page.
   - Draw a thick line across the page.
   - Draw a circle anywhere on the page.
   - Draw a triangle somewhere on the page.
   - ...

   Add directions of your choice that will reinforce art vocabulary. Give students enough time to follow each direction before calling out the next one.

4. When all the directions have been called out, have students compare and contrast their artworks with a partner. How are the pieces the same? How are they different?

5. Display the students' artworks.

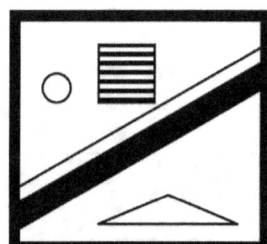 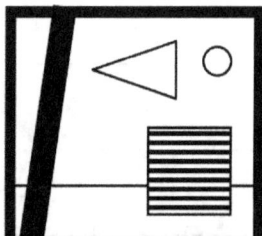 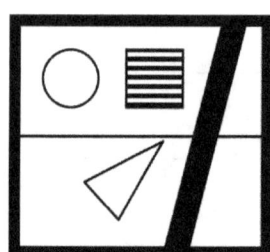 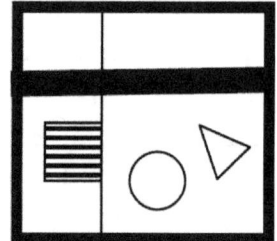

SKETCHBOOK DRAWING IDEAS

Portrait

- Draw a self-portrait. Look at yourself in a mirror for reference.
- Draw a self-portrait of yourself 50 years from now.
- Draw a portrait of a friend or family member. Think about how you can show something about their personality in the portrait.
- Re-create a black and white photograph. Think about the tones in the photograph and how to imitate them.
- Practice drawing different eyes, lips, noses, ears and types of hair. Look through magazines and other materials to find a variety of sizes, shapes and poses.
- Draw a series of portraits of a family member using photographs taken at different stages of their life. For example: baby, child, teenager, adult and senior. Think about what physical characteristics remain constant.
- Practice drawing different parts of the body in various positions. Ask a friend or family member to model arms, legs, heads and shoulders.
- Draw a series of hands in a variety of positions or overlapping them.

Design

- Design a CD cover for your favorite group or singer.
- Design a magazine cover for your favorite magazine.
- Design a logo for your school or a school team.
- Design an advertisement for a vacation destination.
- Design a new cover for a book.
- Design a tattoo for a specific person.
- Design the can for a new drink.
- Design the outside of your dream house.
- Design your ultimate bedroom.
- Design a new stamp.
- Design a new American coin.
- Design a new outfit.
- Design a car.
- Design a new American flag.
- Design a cityscape from the future.

Still Life

- Draw an attractive flower arrangement.
- Draw a plant in great detail.
- Draw a piece of furniture with attention to color, shading and texture.
- Draw a stuffed animal.
- Draw a favorite toy.
- Draw a bowl of fruit.
- Draw an arrangement of three-dimensional figures with attention to shading.

SEASONAL ART IDEAS

FALL

- Paint a fall mural on the classroom windows using a mixture of equal parts dishwashing liquid and paint (use washable liquid paint or powdered tempera paint). Encourage students to add as many details as possible.

- Sketch a still life of a cornucopia, or arrange and sketch a still life of items that represent fall (e.g., fall leaves, corn).

- Make leaf rubbings using chalk and set them with hair spray. Encourage students to arrange and overlap different types of leaves in their rubbings.

- Use black charcoal to draw spooky Halloween pictures.

- Produce beautiful "stained glass" Christmas windows using black construction paper and tissue paper. Students cut out Christmas symbols from the black construction paper, leaving the "window frame." Then students carefully paste different colors of tissue paper to create a stained glass effect.

WINTER

- Paint a winter mural on the classroom windows using a mixture of equal parts dishwashing liquid and paint (use washable liquid paint or powdered tempera paint).

- Draw a winter scene using crayons and apply a wash with salt added, for a snowy effect.

- Draw people in motion participating in various winter sports and activities.

- Make Valentine's Day pendants using self-hardening clay. Students can mold their own shape or use cookie cutters as guides. Paint the pendants with acrylic paint once the clay is dry.

- Go outside on a snowy day and create snow sculptures!

SEASONAL ART IDEAS

SPRING

- Paint a spring mural on the classroom windows using a mixture of equal parts dishwashing liquid and paint (use washable liquid paint or powdered tempera paint).

- Create mosaics using seeds.

- Paper-mache old vases in spring colors. Ask students to bring old vases from home.

- Draw and color realistic pictures of spring flowers. Students should use close-up photographs of flowers as references.

- Draw a still life of an Easter lily arrangement

- Design an Earth Day poster.

- Decorate paper Easter eggs. Students cut egg shapes out of construction paper and draw line patterns on them with water-based markers. Students can trace over the marker lines with white glue to produce an embossed effect (the glue will dry clear).

- Produce beautiful insect and flower "stained glass" windows using black construction paper and tissue paper. Students cut out the desired shapes from the black construction paper, leaving the "window frame." Then students carefully paste different colors of tissue paper to create a stained glass effect.

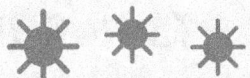 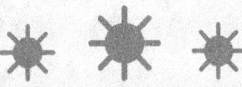

SUMMER

- Paint a summer mural on the classroom windows using a mixture of equal parts dishwashing liquid and paint (use washable liquid paint or powdered tempera paint).

- Make miniature kites. Use straws or wooden craft sticks to construct the frame and cover it with tissue paper. Attach string.

- Draw the outline of a summer scene and fill sections of the drawing using mixed media.

- Draw a still life of beach toys.

- Use oil pastels to draw a still life of a bowl of fruit.

- Build a sandcastle using sand clay. Once the sandcastle is finished, students should gently pat dry sand on the moist clay.

ART RUBRICS

UNDERSTANDING OF ART CONCEPTS RUBRIC

LEVEL	DESCRIPTORS
4	Student shows a thorough understanding of all or almost all concepts and consistently gives appropriate and complete explanations independently. No teacher support is needed.
3	Student shows a good understanding of most concepts and usually gives complete or nearly complete explanations. Infrequent teacher support is needed.
2	Student shows a satisfactory understanding of most concepts and sometimes gives appropriate, but incomplete, explanations. Teacher support is sometimes needed.
1	Student shows little understanding of concepts and rarely gives complete explanations. Intensive teacher support is needed.

COMMUNICATION OF CONCEPTS RUBRIC

LEVEL	DESCRIPTORS
4	Student almost always uses correct art terminology with clarity and precision during class discussions.
3	Student frequently uses correct art terminology during class discussions.
2	Student occasionally uses correct art terminology during class discussions.
1	Student rarely uses correct art terminology during class discussions.

ART RUBRICS

ANALYSIS OF ARTWORKS RUBRIC

LEVEL	DESCRIPTORS
4	Student accurately describes several dominant elements or principles used by the artist. Student accurately describes how they are used by the artist to reinforce the theme, meaning, mood or feeling of the artwork.
3	Student describes without assistance most of the dominant elements and principles used by the artist. Student describes without assistance how these relate to the meaning, mood, theme or feeling of the artwork.
2	Student describes with little assistance some dominant elements and principles used by the artist. Student needs some teacher prompts to describe how these relate to the meaning, mood, theme or feeling of the artwork.
1	Student has difficulty describing the dominant elements and principles used by the artist in the artwork without direct teacher prompts.

INTERPRETATION OF ARTWORKS RUBRIC

LEVEL	DESCRIPTORS
4	Student analyzes and interprets the meaning of the artwork independently using extensive evidence from the artwork.
3	Student analyzes and interprets the meaning of the artwork with occasional teacher prompts using satisfactory evidence from the artwork.
2	Student requires some teacher prompts to analyze and interpret the meaning of the artwork.
1	Student requires direct teacher assistance to analyze and interpret the meaning of the artwork.

ART RUBRICS

CREATIVE WORK RUBRIC

LEVEL	DESCRIPTORS
4	Student applies almost all of the skills, techniques and art concepts taught.
3	Student applies most of the skills, techniques and art concepts taught.
2	Student applies more than half of the skills, techniques and art concepts taught.
1	Student applies fewer than half of the skills, techniques and art concepts taught.

PARTICIPATION RUBRIC

LEVEL	DESCRIPTORS
4	Student consistently contributes to class discussions and activities by offering ideas and asking questions.
3	Student usually contributes to class discussions and activities by offering ideas and asking questions.
2	Student sometimes contributes to class discussions and activities by offering ideas and asking questions.
1	Student rarely contributes to class discussions and activities by offering ideas and asking questions.

CLASS EVALUATION LIST

Student Name	Class Participation	Understanding of Concepts	Communication of Concepts	Analysis of Artworks	Interpretation of Artworks	Creative Work	Overall Evaluation

ART WEB SITES FOR STUDENTS

A. Pintura: Art Detective   http://www.eduweb.com/pintura/

This is a great website that encourages students to become detectives and identify the artist of a mystery painting. By completing the activities students are taught the art concepts of composition, style and subject.

Color Matters   http://www.colormatters.com/

Student artists can see how color affects a person's mind and body, how it is used in design and art, plus lots more. This site explains additive and subtractive color systems, how the eye sees colors, as well as how other cultures view and use colors.

Metropolitan Museum of Art—Kids' Zone

http://www.metmuseum.org/metmedia/kids-zone

Interactive activities and podcasts about art, artists, and world cultures, particularly those featured in the collections of the Met.

Smithsonian American Art Museum

http://americanart.si.edu/education/resources/activities/index.cfm

The "Education" page of the museum's Web site offers links to student activities, including "Zoom It," which allows students to zoom in for a closer look at various areas in a number of works of art.

The National Gallery of Art   http://www.nga.gov/education/index.shtm

The gallery's Web site offers this "Education" page. Explore with students the following links on the page: NGA Classroom: Online Resources for Teachers and Students; NGA Kids; Children's Video Tour.

Origami Fun   http://www.origami-fun.com/printable-origami.html

Students will love experimenting with origami using easy-to-follow printable instructions. Origami projects listed include various flowers, dragon head, talking horse, owl, puffy bunny and much more.

ART GLOSSARY

Abstract art: Art that uses lines, shapes, colors and textures to portray a realistic object in a non-realistic, imaginary way.

Allegory: The use of symbolic figures to represent abstract ideas such as honor and sacrifice.

Analogous colors: Two or more colors that are next to each other on the color wheel. For example: red, red-orange and orange.

Background: The part of the picture plane that seems to be farthest from the viewer.

Balance: A principle of design that deals with arranging the visual elements in a work of art for harmony of design and proportion.

Cast shadow: The shadow created on a surface when an objects blocks the light.

Complementary colors: Colors opposite each other on the color wheel. For example: yellow and purple.

Collage: Creating a picture by gluing pieces of materials such as paper, photos, magazine clippings or found objects to a flat surface.

Color: Color is an element of design. Eyes see color when light bounces off an object. The four characteristics of color are hue, saturation, value and temperature.

Color wheel: A tool for creating and organizing colors and representing relationships among colors.

Comic: A graphic art form in which images and words are used to tell a story. The images are the main focus and are usually presented in strip or page layout.

Composition: Describes the organization of the elements of design used in an artwork.

Contemporary art: Art created by living artists.

Contour drawing: An outline drawing that characterizes the edge of a form. In "blind" contour drawing, an artist slowly draws each curve on the edges of an object without looking at the paper.

Contour lines: Lines that define the edges, ridges, or outline of a shape or form.

Contrast: A principle of design where light colors are used next to dark colors.

ART GLOSSARY

Cool colors: These are the colors that seem to retreat into the background or distance such as green, blue and purple. Colors often associated with cool places, things or feelings.

Elements of design: Color, line, texture, shape and form.

Focal point: The area in an artwork that attracts the viewer's eye as the center of interest.

Foreground: The part of the picture plane which appears closest to the viewer and in front of other objects. The foreground is often at the bottom of a picture.

Form: An element of design describing a three-dimensional object.

Foreshortening: A technique used in perspective to produce the illusion of an object retreating into the background.

Horizon line: A level line where water or land seems to end and the sky begins.

Hue: Another word for color.

Line: An element of design that is used to define shape, contours and outlines. Different lines can suggest a variety of ideas, movements and moods.

Logo: A visual symbol that identifies a business, club, individual or group.

Middle ground: The part of a picture that seems to be in the middle of the picture plane.

Mixed media: Any artwork which uses more than one medium.

Monochromatic: Made using different shades and tints of one color.

Organic shape: Non-geometric or free-flowing shape.

Perspective: The technique used to represent a three-dimensional world (what we see) on a two-dimensional surface (a piece of paper or canvas) in a way that looks realistic. Perspective is used to generate an illusion of space and depth on a flat surface

Pattern: Lines, colors or shapes repeated in a planned way.

Pointillism: A technique of painting, commonly attributed to Georges Seurat, in which tiny dots of color are placed close together. From a distance, the dots seem to disappear and the colors blend.

ART GLOSSARY

Primary colors: The basic colors—red, blue and yellow—from which all other colors can be mixed.

Secondary colors: The colors produced by mixing equal amounts of any two primary colors: blue and red produce purple, yellow and red make orange, and blue and yellow make green.

Sgraffito: A technique created by scratching into paint to reveal the colors underneath.

Shade: Dark value of a color made by adding black.

Shape: An element of design describing the outer form or outline of an image created using line, value, color and/or texture. Shapes may be geometric or organic, positive or negative.

Sketch: A quick drawing that is used as a reference or plan for an artwork.

Space: An element of design that describes the area around, within or between images or other elements of design.

Still life: An artwork depicting a grouping of inanimate objects.

Subject: A topic or idea represented in an artwork.

Symmetry: Symmetry is demonstrated when portions of the object on opposite sides of a line of symmetry are mirror images one of the other.

Tertiary colors: Colors produced by mixing primary colors with secondary colors.

Tint: Light value of a color made by adding white.

Texture: An element of design describing the surface quality of an object.

Wash: Is created by adding water to paint making it thin enough to allow colors applied underneath to show through.

Warm colors: Warm colors are used to make an object seem to advance into the foreground. Red, yellow and orange are warm colors. They suggest warm places, things and feelings.

Value: The lightness or darkness of a color.

Vanishing point: In linear perspective, a position on the horizon where lines or rays between near and distant places appear to come together.

STUDENT ART CERTIFICATES

ARTIST extraordinaire!

Keep up the terrific art!

FANTASTIC ART!

Keep up the great work!